Uniform System of Accounts for the Lodging Industry

Disclaimer

This publication is designed to provide accurate and authoritative information in regard to the subject matter covered. It is sold with the understanding that the publisher is not engaged in rendering legal, accounting, or other professional service. If legal advice or other expert assistance is required, the services of a competent professional person should be sought.

—*From the Declaration of Principles jointly adopted by the American Bar Association and a Committee of Publishers and Associations*

Nothing contained in this publication shall constitute an endorsement by the Educational Institute of the American Hotel & Motel Association (the Institute), the American Hotel & Motel Association (AH&MA), or the Hotel Association of New York City (HANYC) of any information, opinion, procedure, or product mentioned, and the Institute, AH&MA and HANYC disclaim any liability with respect to the use of such information, procedure, or product, or reliance thereon.

Published by
the EDUCATIONAL INSTITUTE of the
AMERICAN HOTEL & MOTEL ASSOCIATION
1407 South Harrison Road
P.O. Box 1240
East Lansing, Michigan 48826

Printed in the United States of America
6 7 8 9 10 11 12 13 14 15 06 05 04 03 02 01 00 99

ISBN 0-86612-128-5

Contents

Preface

The first edition of the *Uniform System of Accounts for Hotels* was published in 1926 by the Hotel Association of New York City. It represented the first successful organized effort to establish a uniform responsibility accounting system for the lodging industry and one of the first such efforts in any industry.

All members of the original committees, appointed by the Hotel Association of New York City to prepare a uniform system of accounts for hotels, deserve commendation for their untiring devotion to the completion of this task. The personnel of these committees were as follows:

Proprietor's Committee

E. M. Statler, Chairman—Hotel Pennsylvania

L. M. Boomer—The Waldorf-Astoria	Julius Manger—Hotel Times Square
I. Fluegelman—12 East 86th Street	Fred A. Muschenheim—Hotel Astor
David H. Knott—Hotel Albert	Charles G. Stamm—Hotel Willard
Arthur L. Lee—Hotel McAlpin	George W. Sweeney—Hotel Commodore

Accountants' Committee

William J. Forster, CPA, Chairman

R. H. Browne .... Hotel McAlpin
W. E. Dodd .... Hotel San Remo
R. E. Frederickson .... Hotel Astor
C. W. Kramer .... Hotel Pennsylvania
E. E. Lightburne .... The Waldorf-Astoria
H. M. Phelps .... The Waldorf-Astoria
W. M. Ross, CPA .... The Biltmore
Thomas E. Ross, CPA .... The Biltmore
R. Schickler .... The Plaza
F. W. Squires, CPA .... Hotel Astor
C. B. Stoner .... Hotels Statler Company Inc.

Accounting Societies

Chester P. Child, CPA, representing N.Y. State Society of CPAs
W. D. Cranstoun, CPA, representing American Institute of Accountants

One of the important results of the work of the Accountants' Committee was the organization of the Hotel Accountants Association of New York City. After the printing of the first edition of the manual, a Manual Committee of the Association was formed, which has been the medium through which the work of the original group has been continued. The Hotel Accountants Association of New York City became the founding chapter of the organization now known as the International Association of Hospitality Accountants. The names of the members of the Committee who worked on previous revisions will be found in the several editions issued since 1926.

At the same time, to meet the needs of its members, the American Hotel & Motel Association appointed the National Association of Accountants in 1961 to develop a uniform system of accounts for small hotels and motels. In 1979 and again in 1986, members of the Committee on Financial Management of the American Hotel & Motel Association revised the original uniform system of accounts for small hotels to reflect the changes in terminology used in the lodging industry. The names of the committee members involved in these publications can be found in the respective editions.

This publication is the product of a subcommittee of the Committee on Financial Management of the American Hotel & Motel Association with representation from the Hotel Association of New York City and the International Association of Hospitality Accountants. The committee members responsible for this edition are:

W. Peter Temling, CPA, Chairman—Carnival Hotels and Casinos

Kapila K. Anand, CPA . . . . KPMG Peat Marwick, LLP
John L. Baldante, CPA . . . . Pannell Kerr Forster PC
George R. Conrade, CHA . . . . Educational Institute of AH&MA
I. Patrick Griggs, CPA, CHAE . . . . Deloitte & Touche, LLP
Howard Isaacson, CPA, CHAE . . . . CapStar Hotels
Larry E. Krause, CPA . . . . Arthur Andersen, LLP
Martin Malk, CPA, CHA . . . . Hotel del Coronado
Richard A. Meza . . . . Chartwell Leisure
Bernard P. Morgan, CPA . . . . Coopers & Lybrand, LLP
Jerome A. Morrison, CPA . . . . Morrison & Company
Gordon Potter, Ph.D. . . . . Cornell University
Raymond Schmidgall, Ph.D., CPA . . . . Michigan State University
Henry A. Weeks, CHAE . . . . The Homestead, Inc.

The committee coordinated its efforts with a committee of the Hotel Association of New York City, which has approved this edition. This comittee consisted of:

Louis N. Ventresca, Chairman . . . . The Sherry-Netherland
Joseph E. Spinnato, President . . . . . Hotel Association of New York City
Fred J. England, Chair—Finance Committee . . . . . . Roger Smith Hotels
Corporation

The committee would like to acknowledge the assistance and contributions of the Technical Committee of the British Association of Hotel Accountants under the chairmanship of Alan Hopper, Pannell Kerr Forster.

This publication is the result of cooperation between the Hotel Association of New York City, which owns the copyright to the publication, and the American Hotel & Motel Association, which has agreed to publish and distribute the work.

American
Hotel & Motel
Association

Changes from the Prior Editions

Major changes in this edition of the Uniform System of Accounts have been made in the following areas:

Overall

The information previously contained in the *Uniform System of Accounts for Hotels, Eighth Revised Edition,* published by the Hotel Association of New York City, and the *Uniform System of Accounts and Expense Dictionary for Small Hotels, Motels, and Motor Hotels,* Fourth Edition, published by the Educational Institute of the American Hotel & Motel Association, has been combined, enhanced, and updated to produce a new, retitled authoritative reference, the *Uniform System of Accounts for the Lodging Industry.*

The new uniform system includes a completely revised and updated Expense Dictionary and Chart of Accounts.

A new section, Ratios and Statistics, has been added. All of the information about various departmental statistics has been brought together in this section, which also includes formulas and explanations for ratios not previously provided.

The information presented about operations budgeting and control has been expanded, and a whole new section on Breakeven Analysis has been added.

Finally, a sample set of statements utilizing the revised uniform system has been included.

Balance Sheet

The descriptions/explanations of all line items appearing in the Balance Sheet have been enhanced. Of particular note, this edition has deleted all references to preopening expenses (although properties that currently have recorded preopening expenses as an asset would continue that amortization until the asset is fully amortized). This action was taken because it has become common practice to write off preopening expenses as incurred or to amortize them over a period of no more than one year. However, it may be acceptable outside the United States to amortize this expense over a number of years. The presentation of investments has been modified to distinguish those held short term or "available-for-sale" under revised accounting pronouncements. New also is a recommendation to write off, over a relatively short period, the initial purchase cost of china, glassware, silver, linen, and uniforms and to expense all replacement purchases. It was felt that this method more closely tracked with the depreciation methods used for furniture and equipment. The balance sheet detail has also been expanded to incorporate details of goodwill and cash surrender value of life insurance. The presentation of deferred income taxes has been modified to allow for the presentation of this item in its various potential locations (assets or liabilities; current or noncurrent) under revised accounting requirements. The owners' equity presentations have also been modified to include presentation of certain items to conform with recent accounting pronouncements.

Statement of Cash Flows

This statement became a required presentation after the last edition of the uniform system was introduced. The suggested formats include examples of both the direct and indirect methods of computing cash from operations.

Departmental Statements of Income

In addition to simplifying the formats used for the departmental statements, there are a number of significant changes and additions. The definition of salaries and wages now also includes the cost of labor when it is contracted for or "leased." In the rooms department, explanations are provided for the treatment of package plans and barter transactions. In the interest of achieving uniformity in reporting information, a decision was also made to include reservation costs only as a rooms department expense. This differs from the prior editions where reservation costs could have been classified as either a rooms department or marketing expense. This decision was made on the basis that the primary purpose of a reservation system is to facilitate the rooms booking function.

The traditional combined food and beverage schedule was split into two schedules, one for food and one for beverage. This action was taken in light of the development and installation of sophisticated electronic registers and point-of-sale devices and the resulting desire and capability to report revenues and expenses by outlet.

A position was also taken to treat banquet service charges as revenue and to record wages paid to banquet staff as part of salary and wages. It was felt that this would ensure accurate reporting and cost analysis.

The separate Guest Entertainment schedule has been excluded from this volume. It was felt that this schedule had little application and, to the extent required, could be accommodated under Other Operated Departments.

In the area of administrative and general, one of the most significant changes made was to reclassify general insurance (i.e., premiums relating to liability, fidelity, and theft coverage) to the "below-the-line" grouping of Rent, Property Taxes, and Insurance. In previous editions, general insurance was charged to administrative and general under the premise that these expenses were related to general operating management of the property. Now, however, in many instances, particularly in managed properties, these costs are controlled by the owner and as such are:

a) not necessarily a function of operations;

b) not controlled by the manager/operator;

c) "owner" expenses, which in managed properties are traditionally classified as fixed charges.

Therefore, general insurance is now included as part of rent, property taxes, and insurance.

In the marketing area, franchise fees have been broken out and listed as a separate line item under Undistributed Operating Expenses. It was felt that the "distribution" throughout the operations statement of various amounts charged by franchisors made uniform presentation difficult. A single location for all such charges allows for comparability.

Another significant change is to include any contracted service expense within the department that is responsible for the contract. For example, contracted service related to the property management system is charged to the rooms department, while a contract to service point-of-sale devices is charged to the food or beverage department. To facilitate recording these expenses, a new expense item, "Contract Services," has been created for each department or cost center.

Because of the role training currently plays and is expected to continue to play in the financial success of a property, it has been added as a new line item in all department schedules.

Less significant are some title changes, including "Telephone" to "Telecommunications," "Data Processing" to "Information Systems," and "Energy Costs" to "Utility Costs."

Another significant addition is the inclusion of a recommended statement for a gaming operation. A schedule for the casino was first included in the seventh edition of the *Uniform System of Accounts for Hotels* published in 1977. The casino schedule was dropped in the eighth edition based upon the recognition that for most establishments with a casino, gaming—not hotel operations—is the primary business. This edition includes a section for gaming for those properties that have a casino, but it is not the primary business.

Introduction

A uniform system of accounts establishes standardized formats and account classifications to guide individuals in the preparation and presentation of financial statements. The recommendations set forth in this uniform system are based on a consensus of senior lodging industry financial executives, public accounting authorities, and leading academic experts, and are consistent with generally accepted accounting principles.

The resulting standardization suggested by the uniform system of accounts permits internal and external users of financial statements to compare the financial position and operational performance of a particular property to similar types of properties in the lodging industry. For new properties just opening, the uniform system of accounts serves as a turnkey accounting system that can be quickly adapted to the needs and requirements of the business.

The *Uniform System of Accounts for the Lodging Industry* is divided into five parts. Part I focuses on the basic financial statements prepared for lodging properties. The first four sections of Part I present the formats and explain the line items on those statements typically produced for external users. These include:

- Balance Sheet
- Statement of Income
- Statement of Owners' Equity
- Statement of Cash Flow

Section 6 of Part I details the format and explains the line items for departmental statements useful in reporting and analyzing operating results. The statements provided apply to full-service lodging properties with food and beverage operations as well as a variety of other services and amenities. Limited-service properties without food and beverage operations should delete those schedules that do not apply to their business.

Likewise, individual properties should adapt the suggested schedules to meet their individual needs and requirements by deleting irrelevant line items and/or adding appropriate line items. However, any changes that individual properties make to the suggested format of the uniform system should be consistent with generally accepted accounting principles. It is also recommended that properties periodically review the format of their financial statements with recognized accounting experts to ensure that their procedures and statements remain in conformity with the pronouncements of the various accounting boards.

Sections 7 and 8 of Part I suggest statements for particular types of operations, namely gaming operations and properties operated by management companies.

The sections of Part II focus on financial analysis and address such areas as:

- Financial Statement Formats

- Ratio Analysis and Statistics
- Breakeven Analysis
- Operations Budgeting and Budgetary Control
- Guidelines for Allocating Expenses to Operated Departments

The last of these sections is the result of a compromise that was made in the development of a uniform system. While some might argue that all expenses should be charged to the department or cost center that is responsible for incurring those expenses, in some cases, doing so would require allocations that could be arbitrary or subjective. Consequently, in the interests of uniformity, a position of not advocating the allocation of indirect or overhead expenses to departments was taken. Only those expenses that can be directly attributed to a particular department are included in the expenses for the department. Section 13 provides some direction, for internal use only, to properties interested in moving toward responsibility accounting.

Part III presents a sample chart of accounts and suggests an approach to bookkeeping that is targeted primarily at small and/or limited-service properties.

Part IV contains the Expense Dictionary, which is designed to help property controllers classify, in accordance with the uniform system, the numerous expense items encountered in their daily work. The Expense Dictionary will also help serve as a ready reference for the executive, the manager, and the purchasing agent, showing them to which account or expense group the accounting department will charge each expense item.

Finally, Part V contains a sample set of uniform system statements. This information will be of particular help to those who would like to see an example of how all of the schedules and statements tie together.

Part I
Financial Statements

A complete set of financial statements includes a Balance Sheet, a Statement of Income, a Statement of Owners' Equity, a Statement of Cash Flows, and Notes to the Financial Statements to amplify the information presented in the basic statements. The Balance Sheet reflects the financial position of a property by detailing the assets, liabilities, and owners' equity as of a given date. The Statement of Income presents revenues and expenses comprising the operations over a given period. The Statement of Owners' Equity summarizes equity transactions over a given period. The Statement of Cash Flows presents cash flow information relating to operating, investing, and financing activities over a given period.

It should be noted that the financial statements discussed in this book and the examples presented have been developed following generally accepted accounting principles. There are comprehensive bases of accounting other than generally accepted accounting principles under which financial statements can be prepared, principally the cash basis and the income tax basis. While the usefulness of such statements is recognized, the principles and practices relating to the preparation of financial statements under these other bases of accounting are beyond the scope of this book.

Section 1
Balance Sheet

The Balance Sheet reflects a balance between a property's assets and the claims to its assets, called liabilities and owners' equity, as of a given date. Assets represent the "things" owned by the property, liabilities represent the claims to the assets by outsiders, and owners' equity represents the claims of the owners to the assets.

The accounts appearing on the Balance Sheet may be arranged in either an account format or a report format. The account format of the Balance Sheet lists the asset accounts on the left side of the page and the liability and the owners' equity accounts on the right side of the page. The report format of the Balance Sheet lists assets, liabilities, and owners' equity in a single column. This arrangement allows the form of the Balance Sheet to reflect either that assets equal liabilities plus owners' equity or that assets minus liabilities equal owners' equity.

An illustration of the account format of the Balance Sheet follows. This illustration includes accounts applicable to many types of lodging properties. Each line item appearing on the Balance Sheet will be explained in the pages that follow.

The number and types of accounts that appear on the Balance Sheet of a property will vary according to the needs and requirements of that property. Accordingly, appropriate modification should be made to the suggested format to accommodate the individual requirements of a property or a business entity, while remaining consistent with generally accepted accounting principles. It is important to remember, however, that similar items should be appropriately grouped and that all significant items should be reflected separately. Significant items are those that are considered material for financial statement purposes.

BALANCE SHEET

Assets

	Current Year	Prior Year
CURRENT ASSETS		
Cash		
House Banks	$	$
Demand Deposits		
Temporary Cash Investments		
Total Cash		
Short-Term Investments		
Receivables		
Accounts Receivable		
Notes Receivable		
Current Maturities of Noncurrent Receivables		
Other		
Total Receivables		
Less Allowance for Doubtful Accounts		
Net Receivables		
Inventories		
Prepaid Expenses		
Deferred Income Taxes, Current		
Other		
Total Current Assets		
NONCURRENT RECEIVABLES, Net of Current Maturities		
INVESTMENTS		
PROPERTY AND EQUIPMENT		
Land		
Leaseholds and Leasehold Improvements		
Furnishings and Equipment		
Buildings		
Construction in Progress		
China, Glassware, Silver, Linen and Uniforms		
Total Property and Equipment		
Less Accumulated Depreciation and Amortization		
Net Property and Equipment		
OTHER ASSETS		
Goodwill		
Cash Surrender Value of Life Insurance		
Deferred Charges		
Deferred Income Taxes—Noncurrent		
Other		
Total Other Assets		
TOTAL ASSETS	$	$

BALANCE SHEET

Liabilities and Owners' Equity

	Current Year	Prior Year
CURRENT LIABILITIES		
Banks	$ _____	$ _____
Others	_____	_____
Total Notes Payable		
Accounts Payable		
Accrued Expenses		
Advance Deposits		
Income Taxes Payable		
Deferred Income Taxes—Current		
Current Maturities of Long-Term Debt		
Other	_____	_____
Total Current Liabilities		
LONG-TERM DEBT, Net of Current Maturities		
Mortgage Notes, other notes, and similar liabilities		
Obligations Under Capital Leases	_____	_____
Total Long-Term Debt		
OTHER LONG-TERM LIABILITIES		
DEFERRED INCOME TAXES—Noncurrent		
COMMITMENTS AND CONTINGENCIES		
OWNERS' EQUITY—one of the formats found on the next page	_____	_____
TOTAL LIABILITIES AND OWNERS' EQUITY	$ ═══	$ ═══

Alternative Owners' Equity Presentations in Balance Sheet

CORPORATION

Stockholders' Equity

	Current Year	Prior Year
____% Cumulative Preferred Stock, $ ____ par value, authorized ____ shares; issued and outstanding ____ shares	$	$
Common Stock, $____ par value, authorized ____ shares; issued and outstanding ____ shares		
Additional Paid-In Capital		
Retained Earnings		
Less: Treasury Stock, ____ shares of Common Stock, at cost	_____	_____
Total Stockholders' Equity	$ _____	$ _____

PARTNERSHIP

Partners' Equity

	Current Year	Prior Year
General Partners	$	$
Limited Partners	_____	_____
Total Partners' Equity	$ _____	$ _____

SOLE PROPRIETORSHIP

	Current Year	Prior Year
Owner's Equity	$ _____	$ _____

ASSETS

Current Assets

This section of the Balance Sheet includes accounts that are to be converted to cash or used in operations within 12 months of the Balance Sheet date. Noncurrent assets (such as Noncurrent Receivables, Property and Equipment, and Other Assets) refer to accounts that are not expected to be converted to cash or used in operations within 12 months of the Balance Sheet date. The accounts appearing under the Current Assets section of the Balance Sheet are commonly listed in the order of their liquidity.

Cash

Cash includes Cash on Hand (House Banks), Demand Deposits, and Temporary Cash Investments. Temporary Cash Investments should be of a demand nature or have maturities within 90 days at the time of purchase. Cash that is restricted formally for long-term purposes, such as for property and equipment replacement reserves, should be included in Noncurrent Assets.

Short-Term Investments

Short-Term Investments are not Temporary Cash Investments, but are intended to be converted to cash or cash equivalents within a year. Short-Term Investments are, essentially, trading securities and should be reflected at market value with the unrealized gain or loss recognized in the Statement of Income. The basis for valuation of such securities should be disclosed in Notes to the Financial Statements.

Receivables

This line item groups Accounts Receivable and Notes Receivable. Based on the needs of the property, a supporting schedule may accompany the Balance Sheet, detailing significant items included within current receivables.

Accounts Receivable. Accounts Receivable consists of the total amount due to the property from accounts carried in the guest, city, and rent ledgers. Accounts due from owners, officers, employees, and affiliated entities should be shown separately, unless insignificant. Accounts not expected to be collected within the next 12 months should be included under Noncurrent Receivables. Significant credit balances should be included in current liabilities under Advance Deposits or Other Liabilities, depending on the nature of the credit balance.

Notes Receivable. Notes Receivable includes notes that are expected to be collected within the next 12 months. Notes Receivable from owners, officers, employees, and affiliated entities should be shown separately, unless insignificant. Notes that are not expected to be collected within the next 12 months should be included under Noncurrent Receivables.

Current Maturities of Noncurrent Receivables. Current Maturities of Noncurrent Receivables includes amounts that are expected to be collected within the next 12 months. Amounts that are not expected to be collected within the next 12 months should be included under Noncurrent Receivables.

Other. Other receivables include those receivables that are not either Accounts or Notes Receivable. Examples include Accrued Interest Receivables and Receivables Due from Employees.

Allowance for Doubtful Accounts. The Allowance for Doubtful Accounts represents an allowance for the portion of current accounts and notes receivable estimated to be uncollectible. The allowance should be based on historical experience, specific appraisal of individual accounts, or other accepted methods. Accounts that become uncollectible should be charged to this account and recoveries of accounts previously written off should be credited to it. The balance at the end of any period, however, should be the best estimate of the portion of accounts and notes receivable that will not be collected.

Inventories

Inventories includes the cost of merchandise held for sale, such as food, beverages, and gift merchandise. This category should also include the cost of reserve stocks of china, glassware, silver, linen and uniforms and of other items such as guest-room supplies. The basis for valuing inventories should be disclosed in Notes to the Financial Statements and, if individual categories are significant in amount, they should be separately stated.

Prepaid Expenses

Prepaid Expenses generally represents payments for items that will benefit future operating periods. Normally, the amounts are charged to operations based upon when the benefits are received. Examples include insurance, property taxes, rent, interest, maintenance, the unused net benefit under barter contracts, and other similar items.

Deferred Income Taxes—Current

Deferred Income Taxes—Current represents the tax effects of temporary differences between the bases of current assets and current liabilities for financial and income tax reporting purposes. For example, if the Allowance for Doubtful Accounts is not deductible for tax purposes until such time as the debt is written off, the Allowance for Doubtful Accounts will result in a current deferred tax asset. Current Deferred Income Taxes are presented as net current assets or net current liabilities as circumstances dictate.

Other

Other current assets include items not shown elsewhere that are reasonably expected to be realized in cash or otherwise in the next 12 months. The category is normally used to capture minor items that are not separately disclosed.

Noncurrent Receivables

Noncurrent Receivables represents accounts and notes that are not expected to be collected during the next 12 months. Amounts due from owners, officers, employees, and affiliated entities should be shown separately, unless insignificant. If any Noncurrent Receivables are estimated to be uncollectible, an Allowance for

Doubtful Noncurrent Receivables should be established utilizing procedures similar to those described under the caption Allowance for Doubtful Accounts.

Investments

Investments generally includes debt or equity securities, whether or not they are traded in recognized markets, and ownership interests that are expected to be held on a long-term basis. Investments in marketable equity securities and debt securities, where there is not the intent and ability to hold such securities to maturity, should be considered "available for sale" and reflected at market value with unrealized gains and losses being shown, net of tax effects, as a separate component of equity. Investment in debt securities where there is the intent and ability to hold such securities to maturity should be considered "held to maturity" and reflected at amortized cost. Investments in affiliated entities should be shown separately, unless insignificant. Investment in entities over which the reporting entity has the ability to exercise significant influence (generally by ownership of more than twenty percent) should be recorded using the equity method. The equity method requires the recording of the investor's share of the investee's income as revenue and an increase in the carrying value of the investment.The method of accounting for and the basis for valuing investments should be disclosed in Notes to the Financial Statements.

Property and Equipment

This grouping of accounts includes owned Land; Buildings; Furnishings and Equipment; China, Glassware, Silver, Linen and Uniforms; and the cost of Leaseholds and Leasehold Improvements. It also includes similar assets held under capital leases. If material, assets held under capital leases should be separately presented on the Balance Sheet or in Notes to the Financial Statements.

Depreciation is a method of allocating the net cost (after reduction for expected salvage value) of the individual assets or classes of assets to operations over their anticipated useful lives. There are several different methods used for depreciation, including straight line, declining balance, and other variants. Under Generally Accepted Accounting Principles, the straight-line method of depreciation is preferred. Declining balance is a method of depreciation usually used for tax depreciation. The number of years chosen for the life of an asset or class of assets also varies somewhat in practice for similar items; however, the methods and the lives used should result in a reasonable allocation of the cost of the assets to operations over their useful lives.

Properties also use a variety of methods to charge the cost of China, Glassware, Silver, Linen and Uniforms to operations. Some properties consider these items part of their inventory and physically count and reflect the aggregate cost of the items on hand. Other properties capitalize the base stock of these items and then expense the cost of items subsequently bought and placed in service. Still other properties initially capitalize the base stock and then depreciate that amount to 50% of the cost over a reasonably short period. These properties take no further depreciation and expense the cost of items subsequently bought and placed in service. While each of the methods has conceptual merit, in order to foster uniformity, a single method is considered preferable. The preferred accounting treatment for China, Glassware, Silver, Linen and Uniforms requires capitalization of the cost of the initial complement of these items. This capitalized cost is then depreciated over a period not to exceed 36 months and replacements are expensed when placed in service. Reserve stocks of these items should be considered inventory until they are placed in service. Major changes in China, Glassware, Silver, Linen and Uniforms, such as when a property changes affiliation and most existing items must be replaced, should be accounted for in a manner similar to the initial complement.

The total Accumulated Depreciation and Amortization should appear as a separate line item. This amount is subtracted from the Total Property and Equipment line to arrive at the Net Property and Equipment line. The methods of depreciation and amortization used by the property should be included in the Notes to the Financial Statements.

Other Assets

Goodwill

Goodwill represents the excess of the purchase price over the fair value of the net assets acquired in the purchase of a business. Goodwill should be amortized over the period during which it is expected to benefit the business. Accumulated Amortization should be shown and the amortization method and period disclosed in the Notes to Financial Statements.

Cash Surrender Value of Life Insurance

Some organizations purchase life insurance on the lives of key individuals. Many of these policies have a cash surrender value that should be recorded as an asset. Changes in the amount of the Cash Surrender Value should be reflected as adjustments to Insurance Expense.

Deferred Charges

Deferred Charges typically relates to financing activities and represent direct costs of obtaining financing such as loan fees and bond issuance costs. Such costs are usually amortized over the life of the related financing. The method and period of amortization should be disclosed in Notes to the Financial Statements.

Deferred Income Taxes—Noncurrent

Deferred Income Taxes—Noncurrent represents the tax effects of temporary differences between the bases of Noncurrent Assets and Noncurrent Liabilities for financial and income tax reporting purposes. For example, if a liability is accrued that will not be paid for an extended period and the expense is deductible only when paid for tax purposes, the accrual will result in a Noncurrent Deferred Income Tax asset. Noncurrent Deferred Income Taxes are presented as net noncurrent assets or net noncurrent liabilities as circumstances dictate.

Other

Noncurrent items that cannot be included under specific groupings such as Security Deposits, Initial Franchise Costs, and other intangible assets should be shown under this caption. Cash balances that are restricted to the acquisition of property and equipment could also be included in this classification. The nature of these items, if material, should be clearly indicated on the Balance Sheet or in the Notes to the Financial Statements. Amortization policies should be disclosed in Notes to the Financial Statements.

LIABILITIES AND OWNERS' EQUITY

Current Liabilities

Notes Payable

Notes Payable includes short-term notes that are payable within the next 12 months, classified on the Balance Sheet as notes due to banks and notes due to other creditors.

Accounts Payable

Accounts Payable represents amounts due to vendors. Amounts due to concessionaires for guest charges collected by the property may be included with Accounts Payable or shown separately.

Accrued Expenses

Accrued Expenses represents expenses incurred but not payable until after the Balance Sheet date. Each item of Accrued Expense, if material, should be listed separately, either on the Balance Sheet or in the Notes to the Financial Statements. Examples include salaries and wages and related benefits, vacation pay, interest, management fees, rent, taxes other than on income, and utilities.

Advance Deposits

Advance Deposits represents amounts received that are to be applied as part of the payment for future sales of rooms and banquets.

Income Taxes Payable

Income Taxes Payable represents the estimated obligations for income taxes.

Deferred Income Taxes—Current

Deferred Income Taxes—Current represents the tax effects of temporary differences between the bases of current assets and current liabilities for financial and income tax reporting purposes. For example, revenue recognized in the financial statements before it is taxable will result in current deferred income taxes if it will be taxable in the next year. Current deferred income taxes are presented as net current assets or net current liabilities as circumstances dictate.

Current Maturities of Long-Term Debt

Current Maturities of Long-Term Debt includes the principal payments of mortgage notes, other notes, and similar liabilities, and the installments on capital leases due within the next 12 months.

Other

Current liabilities not included under other captions should be shown here. The category is normally used to capture minor items that are not separately disclosed. Examples include the unearned portion of amounts received or charged to non-guests for the use of recreational facilities, unredeemed gift certificate sales, un-claimed wages, and the net liability under barter contracts.

Long-Term Debt

This line item includes mortgage notes, other notes, and similar liabilities and obligations under capital leases that are not payable during the next 12 months.

Mortgage Notes

For Mortgage Notes, other notes, and similar liabilities, the following information should be disclosed, either on the Balance Sheet or in Notes to the Financial Statements:

- Interest rates
- Payment or sinking fund requirements
- Maturity dates
- Collateralization and assets pledged
- Financial restrictive covenants
- Payment and sinking fund payments required for each of the five years subsequent to the Balance Sheet date

Obligations Under Capital Leases

For Obligations Under Capital Leases, disclosure should be made of the future minimum lease payments for each of the five years subsequent to the Balance Sheet date and the total future minimum lease obligations, with a deduction for the imputed interest necessary to reduce the net minimum lease payments to present value.

Other Long-Term Liabilities

Long-term liabilities, being liabilities that will not require satisfaction within a year, that are not included under other captions should be included here. Examples include Deferred Compensation, Deferred Management Fees and Tenants' Lease Deposits, and accrued obligations for pension and other post-employment bene-fits. The nature of these items, if material, should be clearly indicated on the Bal-ance Sheet or in the Notes to the Financial Statements.

Deferred Income Taxes—Noncurrent

Deferred Income Taxes—Noncurrent represents the tax effects of temporary differ-ences between the bases of Noncurrent Assets and Noncurrent Liabilities for finan-cial and income tax reporting purposes. For example, the use of accelerated depreciation for tax purposes and straight-line depreciation for financial reporting purposes will result in noncurrent deferred income taxes. Noncurrent deferred income taxes are presented as net noncurrent assets or net noncurrent liabilities as circumstances dictate.

Commitments and Contingencies

The Commitments and Contingencies caption is indicated on the Balance Sheet only to bring the reader's attention to such items. No dollar amounts should be shown on the Balance Sheet. Adequate disclosure of all significant commitments and contingencies should be made in the Notes to the Financial Statements. Examples include commitments for purchase contracts, employment contracts, long-term leases, and management agreements and contingencies for pending or threatened litigation and guarantees of indebtedness of others.

OWNERS' EQUITY

The Owners' Equity section of the Balance Sheet is presented differently for corporations, partnerships, and sole proprietorships, depending upon the type of equity ownership. Balance Sheet presentation formats are shown on page 6. Examples of detailed presentations of Statements of Owners' Equity are shown in Section 3.

Corporation

Stockholders' Equity

Capital Stock. Capital Stock denotes the shares of ownership of a corporation that have been authorized by its articles of incorporation. The most prevalent classes of Capital Stock are Preferred and Common Stock. The par or stated value and the number of shares authorized and issued for each class of stock should be presented on the Balance Sheet. Changes during the period should be shown in the Statement of Stockholders' Equity.

Additional Paid-In Capital. Additional Paid-In Capital includes cash, property, and other capital contributed to a corporation by its shareholders in excess of the stated or par value of Capital Stock. Changes during the period should be shown in the Statement of Stockholders' Equity.

Retained Earnings. Retained Earnings represents the accumulated Net Income not distributed as dividends but retained in the business. Changes during the period should be shown in the Statement of Stockholders' Equity. Negative Retained Earnings are generally referred to as deficits.

Treasury Stock. Treasury Stock represents the cost of the company's stock acquired by the company and not retired, and should be reflected as a reduction in total Stockholders' Equity. Changes during the period should be shown in the Statement of Stockholders' Equity.

Partnership

Partners' Equity

Partners' Equity represents the net equity of the partners in the partnership and should be classified where appropriate as general and limited partners' equity. Changes during the period should be shown in the Statement of Partners' Equity.

Contributions. Contributions include the amount of any additional assets that are invested in the business by the partners during the period just ended.

Withdrawals. Withdrawals include the amount of any assets that are taken out of the business and distributed to the partners during the period just ended.

Sole Proprietorship

Owner's Equity

The Owner's Equity of a sole proprietorship is similar to the equity of a partnership except that it represents the interest of one individual as opposed to a number of partners. Changes during the period should be shown in the Statement of Owner's Equity.

Contributions. Contributions include the amount of any additional assets that are invested in the business by the owner during the period just ended.

Withdrawals. Withdrawals include the amount of any assets that are taken out of the business and distributed to the owner during the period just ended.

Unrealized Gains or Losses on Investments

Cumulative Unrealized Gains or Losses on Investments are not presented in the illustrated Owners' Equity section of the Balance Sheet; however, entities that have investments held for sale, other than trading securities, are required to reflect those investments at market value with the resulting Unrealized Gain or Loss as of the Balance Sheet date shown as a separate component in the Owners' Equity section of the Balance Sheet. The amount is reflected net of income tax implications. This presentation is illustrated in Section 3.

Cumulative Foreign Currency Translation Adjustments

Cumulative Foreign Currency Translation Adjustments are not presented in the illustrated Owners' Equity section of the Balance Sheet; however, entities that include foreign operations in their financial statements by translating the foreign entities' assets and liabilities at the current exchange rates should account for the cumulative effects of such translations by adding a separate component in the Owners' Equity section of the Balance Sheet.

Format of Accounts Outside the United States

The examples and formats used throughout this book follow U.S. accounting standards for the presentation of financial statements. Users of the book outside the

United States should be aware that the accounting requirements of their own jurisdictions will not necessarily follow those of the United States. The laws of other jurisdictions and the application of accounting standards may significantly affect the format and presentation of financial statements.

For example, countries that are Member States of the European Union must follow the layout prescribed for company accounts in the European Fourth Directive on Company Accounts—a layout that is quite different from the U.S. standard. Other jurisdictions have no legal requirements and so whatever layout is considered most appropriate in those circumstances may be used.

Section 2
Statement of Income

The Statement of Income reflects the results of operations for a period of time. The time covered by this statement usually ends at the Balance Sheet date. When the statement reflects a net loss, the title is generally changed to Statement of Operations.

Hospitality organizations prepare income statements for both external users (e.g., potential investors, creditors, and owners not active in managing the business) and internal users (i.e., managers of the business). These statements differ in the amount of information presented. The statement presented to external users is relatively brief, providing only summary detail about the results of operations.

Two sample formats for external users are shown here. The degree of detail presented in the statements is somewhat discretionary although the following captions—revenue, expenses, interest, depreciation, and income taxes—should be presented unless the amounts are insignificant. To the extent that any individual revenue or expense item is significant, separate disclosure should be made. (For Securities and Exchange Commission purposes, a hotel/casino should present three revenue categories: Rooms, Food and Beverage, and Casino.) A format useful for managers operating the property is discussed in Section 6.

STATEMENT OF INCOME		
	Period	
	Current Year	**Prior Year**
REVENUE		
Rooms	$	$
Food		
Beverage		
Other	————	————
Total Revenue		
COSTS AND EXPENSES		
Rooms		
Food		
Beverage		
Administrative and General		
Interest Expense		
Depreciation and Amortization	————	————
Total Costs and Expenses	————	————
INCOME BEFORE INCOME TAXES		
INCOME TAXES		
Current		
Deferred	————	————
Total Income Taxes	————	————
NET INCOME	$ ————	$ ————

STATEMENT OF INCOME

	Period	
	Current Year	**Prior Year**
REVENUE		
Rooms	$	$
Food		
Beverage		
Telecommunications		
Garage and Parking		
Other Operated Departments		
Rentals and Other Income	———	———
Total Revenue		
COSTS AND EXPENSES		
Rooms		
Food		
Beverage		
Telecommunications		
Garage and Parking		
Other Operated Departments		
Administrative and General		
Human Resources		
Information Systems		
Security		
Marketing		
Franchise Fees		
Transportation		
Property Operation and Maintenance		
Utility Costs		
Management Fees		
Rent, Property Taxes, and Insurance		
Interest Expense		
Depreciation and Amortization	———	———
Total Costs and Expenses		
INCOME BEFORE INCOME TAXES		
INCOME TAXES		
Current		
Deferred	———	———
Total Income Taxes	———	———
NET INCOME	$ ———	$ ———

Section 3
Statement of Owners' Equity

A separate Statement of Owners' Equity should be presented if there is significant activity in the accounts during the period. If net income or loss is the only change to the equity accounts in the period, it is permissible to reconcile the change in retained earnings at the bottom of the Statement of Income and exclude presentation of the separate owners' equity statement. The format of the owners' equity statement will depend on the type of entity. The following pages show examples of the type of presentation for corporations, partnerships, and sole proprietorships.

STATEMENT OF STOCKHOLDERS' EQUITY

	Preferred Stock		Common Stock				Treasury Stock			
	Number of Shares Outstanding	Amount	Number of Shares Outstanding	Amount	Additional Paid-in Capital	Retained Earnings	Number of Shares	Amount	Unrealized Gain (Loss) on Marketable Securities[1]	Total Stockholders' Equity
BALANCE AT BEGINNING OF PRIOR YEAR		$		$	$	$		$	$	$
Add (Deduct)										
Net Income										
Dividends Declared										
Change in Unrealized Gains (Losses)										
Net Proceeds from Sale of Stock										
Treasury Stock Acquired										
Other										
BALANCE AT END OF PRIOR YEAR		$		$	$	$		$	$	$
Add (Deduct)										
Net Income										
Dividends Declared										
Change in Unrealized Gains (Losses)										
Net Proceeds from Sale of Stock										
Treasury Stock Acquired										
Other										
BALANCE AT END OF CURRENT YEAR		$		$	$	$		$	$	$

[1]Unrealized gain or loss on marketable securities held for sale is reflected net of related income taxes.

Cumulative foreign currency translation adjustments should also be reflected in this statement.

STATEMENT OF PARTNERS' EQUITY

	General Partners	Limited Partners	Unrealized Gain (Loss) on Marketable Securities[1]	Total
BALANCE AT BEGINNING OF PRIOR YEAR	$	$	$	$
Add (Deduct)				
Net Income				
Contributions				
Change in Unrealized Gains (Losses)				
Withdrawals				
Other				
BALANCE AT END OF PRIOR YEAR	$	$	$	$
Add (Deduct)				
Net Income				
Contributions				
Change in Unrealized Gains (Losses)				
Withdrawals				
Other				
BALANCE AT END OF CURRENT YEAR	$	$	$	$

[1]Unrealized gain or loss on marketable securities held for sale is reflected net of related income taxes.

Cumulative foreign currency translation adjustments should also be reflected in this statement.

STATEMENT OF OWNER'S EQUITY

	Owner	Unrealized Gain (Loss) on Marketable Securities[1]	Total
BALANCE AT BEGINNING OF PRIOR YEAR	$	$	$
Add (Deduct)			
Net Income			
Contributions			
Change in Unrealized Gains (Losses)			
Withdrawals			
Other			
BALANCE AT END OF PRIOR YEAR	$	$	$
Add (Deduct)			
Net Income			
Contributions			
Change in Unrealized Gains (Losses)			
Withdrawals			
Other			
BALANCE AT END OF CURRENT YEAR	$	$	$

[1]Unrealized gain or loss on marketable securities held for sale is reflected net of related income taxes.

Cumulative foreign currency translation adjustments should also be reflected in this statement.

Section 4
Statement of Cash Flows

The Statement of Cash Flows summarizes the change in Cash and Temporary Cash Investments over the same period of time as that covered by the Statement of Income. Temporary Cash Investments are readily convertible investments with a maturity of less than three months at the time of purchase. The change in Cash and Temporary Cash Investments is classified as being derived from three activities: operating, investing, and financing.

Cash flows from operating activities represent the amount of cash generated by property operations. Operating activities include transactions involving acquiring, selling, and delivering goods for sale, as well as providing services. Cash flows from operating activities for a property include cash collected from customers, cash paid to employees and other suppliers, interest paid and received, taxes paid, and other operating payments and receipts. Cash from operating activities measures the amount that net income would have been if the cash method were used for measuring revenues and expenses.

Cash flows from investing activities represent changes in cash arising from transactions related to asset accounts that do not affect operations. Transactions include acquisition and disposal of property and facilities as well as the purchase and sale of investments, whether they are current or noncurrent.

Cash flows from financing activities represent cash changes related to liability and equity accounts that do not affect operations. These include obtaining and repaying debt (whether current or noncurrent), issuing and repurchasing stock, and dividend payments.

Cash flows from operating activities can be computed using either the direct or indirect approach. The direct method identifies the operating cash receipts and cash disbursements. The indirect approach determines the cash from operations by adjusting net income for noncash items. The indirect approach is useful for identifying why net income differs from cash from operating activities. The direct approach is easier to interpret as it specifically identifies the cash inflows and outflows from operations.

If the direct method of presentation is used, a summarized reconciliation of the significant items comprising the difference between net income and cash flows from operating activities should also be presented.

While the Statement of Cash Flows summarizes all significant sources and uses of cash, there is also a requirement to disclose significant noncash investing and financing activities. This information is generally presented in narrative form immediately below the Statement. Items that should be disclosed include the purchase of capital assets by incurring debt or through capital lease transactions. Transactions involving the sale of assets where the seller provides financing is another example requiring disclosure.

Direct Method

Statement of Cash Flows

	Period	
	Current Year	Prior Year
CASH FLOWS FROM OPERATING ACTIVITIES		
Guest Receipts	$	$
Other Receipts		
Payroll Disbursements		
Other Operating Disbursements		
Interest Paid		
Income Taxes Paid		
Franchise Fees Paid		
Management Fees Paid		
Net Cash Provided By (Used In) Operating Activities		
CASH FLOWS FROM INVESTING ACTIVITIES		
Capital Expenditures		
Decrease (Increase) in Restricted Cash		
Proceeds from Asset Dispositions		
Proceeds from Sale of Investments		
Purchases of Investments		
Net Cash Provided By (Used In) Investing Activities		
CASH FLOWS FROM FINANCING ACTIVITIES		
Proceeds from Debt or Equity Financing		
Debt Repayments		
Dividends Paid		
Distribution to Owners/Partners		
Net Cash Provided By (Used In) Financing Activities		
INCREASE (DECREASE) IN CASH AND TEMPORARY CASH INVESTMENTS		
CASH AND TEMPORARY CASH INVESTMENTS, BEGINNING OF PERIOD		
CASH AND TEMPORARY CASH INVESTMENTS, END OF PERIOD	$	$
CASH PAID FOR INTEREST		
CASH PAID FOR INCOME TAXES		
SUPPLEMENTAL INFORMATION RELATED TO NONCASH INVESTING AND FINANCING ACTIVITIES (DISCLOSE SIGNIFICANT ITEMS SEPARATELY.)		

Cash Flows from Operating Activities

Guest Receipts

Guest Receipts includes all receipts from guest-related activities including those applicable to unearned income.

Indirect Method

Statement of Cash Flows

	Period	
	Current Year	Prior Year
CASH FLOWS FROM OPERATING ACTIVITIES		
Net Income	$	$
Adjustments to Reconcile Net Income		
To Cash Provided By (Used In) Operating Activities:		
Depreciation and Amortization		
Loss (Gain) on Sale of Property and Equipment		
Deferred Taxes		
Decrease (Increase) in Accounts Receivable		
Decrease (Increase) in Inventory		
Decrease (Increase) in Prepaids		
Increase (Decrease) in Payables		
Increase (Decrease) in Accruals	_____	_____
Net Cash Provided By (Used In) Operating Activities		
CASH FLOWS FROM INVESTING ACTIVITIES		
Capital Expenditures		
Decrease (Increase) in Restricted Cash		
Proceeds from Asset Dispositions		
Proceeds from Sale of Investments		
Purchases of Investments	_____	_____
Net Cash Provided By (Used In) Investing Activities		
CASH FLOWS FROM FINANCING ACTIVITIES		
Proceeds from Debt or Equity Financing		
Debt Repayments		
Dividends Paid		
Distribution to Owners/Partners	_____	_____
Net Cash Provided By (Used In) Financing Activities		
INCREASE (DECREASE) IN CASH AND TEMPORARY CASH INVESTMENTS		
CASH AND TEMPORARY CASH INVESTMENTS, BEGINNING OF PERIOD	_____	_____
CASH AND TEMPORARY CASH INVESTMENTS, END OF PERIOD	$_____	$_____
CASH PAID FOR INTEREST		
CASH PAID FOR INCOME TAXES		

SUPPLEMENTAL INFORMATION RELATED TO NONCASH INVESTING AND FINANCING ACTIVITIES (DISCLOSE SIGNIFICANT ITEMS SEPARATELY)

Other Receipts

Other Receipts includes proceeds from transactions other than with guests; for example, from casual sales of furnishings, salvage, interest and dividends received, and other activities.

Payroll Disbursements

Payroll Disbursements includes salary and wage payments as well as related payments for employee benefits.

Other Operating Disbursements

Other Operating Disbursements includes payments for food and beverage, other merchandise and supplies, energy, rent, taxes other than income, and other expenditures incurred by operations.

Interest Paid

Interest Paid includes cash payments to lenders and other creditors for interest. The amount should be shown net of interest capitalized.

Income Taxes Paid

Income Taxes Paid includes all payments for taxes based on income. It does not include amounts paid for sales or occupancy taxes.

Franchise and Management Fees Paid

Franchise and Management Fees Paid includes the base as well as variable elements paid under franchise and management contracts.

Cash Flows from Investing Activities

Capital Expenditures

Capital Expenditures represents payments to purchase property, buildings, equipment, and other productive assets. These payments include interest payments capitalized as part of the cost of those assets. A separate disclosure may be appropriate for the portion of the capital expenditures that results in an increase in the revenue-generating capacity of the lodging property. Separating cash payments that represent an increase in revenue-generating capacity from cash payments that are required to maintain operating capacity is helpful in enabling users to determine whether the lodging property is investing adequately in the maintenance of its operating capacity.

Decrease (Increase) in Restricted Cash

The change in the noncurrent restricted cash is included in this item. The change represents the difference between the additional cash set aside or restricted and the use of those funds for the restricted purpose.

Proceeds from Asset Dispositions

The Proceeds from Asset Dispositions, reduced by selling cost payments, are included in this item. This item should not include any amount of the sales consideration that has been financed by the seller.

Proceeds from Sale of Investments

The net Proceeds from the Sale of Investments, after deduction of selling expenses, should be included in this item.

Purchases of Investments

The purchase price paid for investments, including the transaction costs paid, should be included in this item.

Cash Flows from Financing Activities

Proceeds from Debt or Equity Financing

The net proceeds after deduction of transaction costs should be included in this item. Separate captions should be shown if amounts are significant. This item includes long- and short-term financing.

Debt Repayments

Aggregate principal repayments on indebtedness should be included in this item.

Dividends and Distributions Paid

The amount of Dividends Paid to owners should be included. Other distributions to owners should be included, with appropriate modification of the caption, if the entity is not a corporation.

Section 5
Notes to the Financial Statements

In order for a financial presentation to be complete, the financial statements should be accompanied by explanatory notes. The notes should describe all significant accounting policies followed by the organization. Commonly required disclosures include, but are not limited to, policies regarding the following:

- Basis of consolidation

- Use of estimates

- Cash and temporary cash investments

- Inventory methods and valuation

- Accounting for investments, including the valuation of marketable securities

- Depreciation and amortization policies

- Amortization of intangibles

- Accounting for deferred charges

- Advertising costs

- Accounting for pensions

- Recognition of income from franchising or leasing operations

- Accounting for income taxes

- Computation of net income (loss) per share (only public companies)

Disclosure of accounting policy-related footnotes should be followed by such additional notes as are necessary to provide for full disclosure of all significant events or conditions reflected in the financial statements, or as otherwise required by the rules of professional accounting or regulatory organizations. Typical events and conditions which are disclosed in the notes accompanying financial statements include the following:

- Changes in accounting methods

- Long-term debt agreements

- Pension and/or profit-sharing plans

- Other post-retirement and post-employment benefits

- Income taxes

- Long-term contracts

- Stock option plans

- Extraordinary items of income or expense
- Significant long-term commitments, including leases
- Foreign operations
- Related party transactions
- Contingent liabilities, including pending litigation
- Subsequent events
- Stockholders' equity transactions
- Financial instruments

Section 6
Departmental Statements

The Departmental Statements of Income reflect the results of operations for a given period. They provide some of the most important internal sources of information for lodging property managers.

It is suggested that an overall Summary Statement of Income be prepared with supporting schedules of revenues and expenses for each of the departments or activities in the property. The Summary Statement of Income, shown on page 33, is divided into several sections. The Operated Departments section of the Summary Statement of Income reports the Net Revenue, Cost of Sales, Payroll and Related Expenses, Other Expenses, and Income (Loss) for all major revenue-producing departments of the property.

The Undistributed Operating Expenses section of the Summary Statement of Income reports expenses that are considered applicable to the entire property and are not easily allocated to operated departments.

Income After Undistributed Operating Expenses is calculated by subtracting Total Undistributed Operating Expenses from the Income (Loss) of the Total Operated Departments.

Management Fees represents the cost of using an independent management company to operate the property. The remaining expenses are associated with owning or leasing property, facilities, or equipment. These include: Rent, Property Taxes, and Insurance; Interest Expense; and Depreciation and Amortization. Management Fees and Rent, Property Taxes, and Insurance are subtracted from Income After Undistributed Operating Expenses to arrive at Income Before Depreciation, Amortization, and Income Taxes. Depreciation and Amortization is subtracted from the previously calculated amount as the first step to determine Income Before Income Taxes.

On the Summary Statement of Income, gains on sale of property are reported separately from revenues, and losses on sale of property are reported separately from expenses, because these distinctions are important in evaluating the effectiveness of management. Management is primarily held responsible for revenues and expenses associated with operations, and only secondarily (if at all) for gains and losses on the sale of property. Gains are added and losses are subtracted to determine Income Before Income Taxes. Finally, Income Taxes are subtracted to determine Net Income.

The number and types of Operated Departments and Undistributed Operating Expenses will vary according to the needs and requirements of individual properties. The Summary Statement of Income shown on page 33 presents an extensive list of Operated Departments for a full-service property with a wide range of recreational offerings. Therefore, the line items listed on the Summary Statement of Income presented here may not apply to most small properties.

Individual properties should modify the Summary Statement of Income to meet their own needs and requirements.

Sample supporting schedules and explanations of line items appearing on them are presented in the pages that follow. The supporting schedule numbers are for cross-reference purposes only.

A sample set of uniform system statements is presented in Part V. The suggested statements are presented for guidance only, because it is recognized that it would be impractical to prescribe a single model for every possible situation. The accounting presentation and disclosure in each set of financial statements should include the information necessary in the particular circumstances.

SUMMARY STATEMENT OF INCOME

	Schedule	Net Revenues	Cost of Sales	Payroll and Related Expenses	Other Expenses	Income (Loss)
Operated Departments		$	$	$	$	$
Rooms	1					
Food	2					
Beverage	3					
Telecommunications	4					
Garage and Parking	5					
Golf Course	6					
Golf Pro Shop	7					
Guest Laundry	8					
Health Center	9					
Swimming Pool	10					
Tennis	11					
Tennis Pro Shop	12					
Other Operated Departments	13					
Rentals and Other Income	14					
Total Operated Departments						
Undistributed Operating Expenses[1]						
Administrative and General	15					
Human Resources	16					
Information Systems	17					
Security	18					
Marketing	19					
Franchise Fees	19a					
Transportation	20					
Property Operation and Maintenance	21					
Utility Costs	22					
Total Undistributed Operating Expenses						
Totals		$	$	$	$	
Income After Undistributed Operating Expenses						
Management Fees	23					
Rent, Property Taxes, and Insurance	24					
Income Before Interest, Depreciation and Amortization, and Income Taxes[2]						
Interest Expense	25					
Income Before Depreciation, Amortization and Income Taxes						
Depreciation and Amortization	26					
Gain or Loss on Sale of Property						
Income Before Income Taxes						
Income Taxes	27					
Net Income					$

(1)A separate line for preopening expenses can be included if such costs are captured separately.
(2)Also referred to as EBITDA—Earnings before Interest, Taxes, Depreciation and Amortization

ROOMS

```
                        Rooms—Schedule 1

                                                    Current Period

 REVENUE                                            $

 ALLOWANCES                                         _____

 NET REVENUE

 EXPENSES
    Salaries and Wages
    Employee Benefits                               _____
       Total Payroll and Related Expenses          _____
    Other Expenses
       Cable/Satellite Television
       Commissions
       Complimentary Guest Services
       Contract Services
       Guest Relocation
       Guest Transportation
       Laundry and Dry Cleaning
       Linen
       Operating Supplies
       Reservations
       Telecommunications
       Training
       Uniforms
       Other
          Total Other Expenses                     _____
                                                   _____
 TOTAL EXPENSES                                    _____

 DEPARTMENTAL INCOME (LOSS)                         $ _____
```

Rooms—Schedule 1 illustrates a format and identifies line items that commonly appear on a supplemental schedule supporting the Net Revenue, Payroll and Related Expenses, Other Expenses, and Income (Loss) amounts reported on the Summary Statement of Income for Operated Departments—Rooms. This format and the line items will vary according to the needs and requirements of individual properties. Therefore, the line items listed on Schedule 1 may not apply to the operations of every property. Individual properties should modify Schedule 1 to meet their own needs and requirements.

Revenue

Rooms Revenue includes revenue derived from rooms and suites rented or leased for part of a day, a week, a month, or longer. Some properties break down rooms revenue in terms of Transient, Permanent, and Other. "Transient" revenue commonly includes revenue derived from rooms and suites rented or leased for part of a day, a full day, a week, or a month by individual travelers or by groups of travelers. "Permanent" revenue includes revenue derived from rooms and suites rented or leased to guests who have established residence in the property for an extended period; a formal contract may or may not exist. Revenue from rooms sold to specific groups on a contracted basis, such as airline crews or corporate use, should be considered transient revenue. "Other" revenue includes revenue derived from the rental of guestrooms and suites for day use rentals.

The proliferation of computers and the need for significantly additional information to design, implement, and evaluate sophisticated marketing programs has increased the prevalence of identifying rooms revenue by market source. While the particular categories will vary from property to property, the information is generally segregated between group business and that related to individuals. Market segments that might be segregated include the following:

- Groups
  - Corporate
  - Associations/conventions
  - Government
  - Tour groups
    - Domestic
    - Foreign
  - Airline Crews
  - SMERF—Social, Military, Educational, Religious, Fraternal
- Individuals
  - Business
  - Leisure
  - Preferred
  - Travel packages
  - Hotel packages
  - Discounts

Allocation of Packaged Revenues

Sometimes guests are sold accommodations in conjunction with other services provided by either the property or third parties. For instance, a guest might receive accommodations and food or other services in a single transaction. Alternatively, a guest could obtain accommodations and a rental vehicle for a single price. Golf packages, where accommodations and golf privileges are provided for a combined price, are another example. Care should be taken to ensure that revenues are appropriately allocated between departments or third party vendors in these situations.

In the case where interdepartmental allocations are necessary (for example, where revenues have to be allocated between the rooms and the food and beverage departments), it is recommended that the allocation be made based on the notional "market" values for the separate services. The "market" values should represent average realized amounts achieved by the property for similar services. The packaged revenue will then be allocated based on the ratio between these market values.

As an example, consider the following package consisting of a guestroom for the night, two meals, and the use of the resort's spa facilities at an inclusive price of $120. The resort computes the departmental allocations as follows:

	Market Value	Ratio	Package Allocations
Rooms	$100	50%	$60
Food	70	35%	42
Spa	30	15%	18
	$200	100%	$120

It is also suggested that the ratio be used on a consistent basis and modified only when the notional values are estimated to have changed significantly.

In the case of packages that include a third party vendor, the rate for the provision of the third party service will likely be established by the contractual arrangement. The amount that the third party will receive should not be reflected as revenue.

Sales and Excise Taxes and Transient Occupancy Taxes

Many jurisdictions levy sales or excise taxes on revenues. In addition, certain jurisdictions assess a transient occupancy, value added, or accommodations tax on certain lodging revenues. In some cases, the lodging facility merely acts as a conduit in the collection of taxes for the taxing authority because the amount of the tax collected from the guest is remitted to the taxing authority. In other cases, the facility is required to pay the taxes to the taxing authority regardless of whether the tax is charged to the customers. In practice, the accounting for both these types of taxes is generally the same. The taxes assessed to guests are credited to a payable account and no revenue is recognized.

Frequent Stay Programs

In an attempt to build customer loyalty and repeat business, some facilities and chains have implemented frequent stay programs where low priced or free accommodations or services are provided to frequent guests based on various levels of patronage. The form and details of these programs are many and varied. Generally, however, it is recommended that the "cost" of providing frequent stay points be recognized as a marketing expense at the time of the paying guest's visit and that the offsetting revenue be reflected in rooms when the guests utilize their accumulated benefits. It is recommended that the "value" assigned to the benefit be a conservative average of the market rate for similar accommodations or services at the property.

No Shows

Revenue from guests who guaranteed their arrival but did not show should be included in rooms department revenue when collection is reasonably assured.

Barter Transactions

Lodging properties often enter into barter transactions. Typically, these arrangements require the property to provide accommodations and possibly food, beverages, golf packages, and other services in exchange for other services, such as advertising. These are nonmonetary transactions that are settled through the provision of goods and services. The form and details of barter transactions vary; however, it should be borne in mind that barter arrangements would seldom be necessary or attractive if high levels of premium-paying guests were available. The value assigned to the services received should, accordingly, be a conservative average of the market rate for similar accommodations or services at the property.

At the outset, barter transactions are executory arrangements that require no recognition. It is suggested, however, that the internal records of the property reflect the barter obligation and the unused barter asset at the time the contract is negotiated. Services provided by the property are then reflected in revenues and charged to the obligation, and services received by the property are charged to expense and credited to the unused asset. For external reporting purposes, the remaining obligation and unused asset should be netted and reflected as a single amount in either the current assets or the current liabilities. Obviously, the net unused position at the end of the contract period should be reflected in revenue or expense, as appropriate.

Allowances

Allowances includes rebates, refunds, and overcharges of revenue not known at the time of sale but adjusted at a later date.

Net Revenue

Net Revenue is calculated by subtracting Allowances from Total Revenue. The Net Revenue amount is the same amount that appears on the Summary Statement of Income in the Net Revenues column for Operated Departments—Rooms.

Expenses

Salaries and Wages

Salaries and Wages includes regular pay, overtime pay, vacation pay, sick pay, holiday pay, incentive pay, severance pay, and bonuses for employees of the rooms department. This line item should also include any expense associated with leased labor, but not contract labor, which should be charged to Contract Services. If leased labor expense is significant, a separate line item called Leased Labor should be created and listed immediately after Salaries and Wages. For a classification of employees included in the rooms department, see Salaries and Wages, Schedule 29.

Employee Benefits

Employee Benefits includes payroll taxes, payroll-related insurance expense, pension, and other payroll-related expenses applicable to the rooms department. The cost of meals furnished to employees whose salaries and wages are charged to the rooms department is also included in this expense item. (See Payroll Taxes and Employee Benefits, Schedule 30.)

Total Payroll and Related Expenses

Total Payroll and Related Expenses is calculated by adding Salaries and Wages to Employee Benefits. The Total Payroll and Related Expenses amount is the same amount that appears on the Summary Statement of Income in the Payroll and Related Expenses column for Operated Departments—Rooms.

Other Expenses

This expense grouping includes significant rooms department expenses. Items appearing under Other Expenses vary from property to property. Examples of items that commonly appear as Other Expenses follow.

Cable/Satellite Television. Cable/Satellite Television includes the cost of providing cable and satellite video services to guestrooms. It does not include the cost associated with pay-per-view movies.

Commissions. Commissions includes remuneration paid to authorized agents for securing rooms business for the property, such as travel agents' commissions. Travel agents are often a significant source of business for the lodging industry. Travel agent commissions are generally reflected as an expense of the rooms department regardless of whether the commission relates to accommodations only or to other services as well. This practice is generally followed because allocation of these commissions to other departments would not be cost effective.

In certain circumstances, volume discounts are given to travel agents and other significant guest providers based on the level of business provided. It is recommended that such volume discounts be recorded as a reduction from rooms revenue (representing a reduction on the revenue recorded for the business) rather than as a charge to the commission expense account.

In other situations, blocks of rooms are provided to wholesalers and jobbers on a substantially discounted basis. These rooms are subsequently remarketed by the wholesalers and jobbers to the eventual guest. It is suggested that these sales be recorded as revenue at the negotiated rate and that no attempt be made to record additional revenue based on a notional or normal commission rate with an offset to commission expense.

Commissions also includes remuneration paid to rental agents for permanent rooms business that may involve leases. In the case of leases, the remuneration is prorated over the term of the lease.

Complimentary Guest Services. Complimentary Guest Services includes the cost of providing food and beverages to guests on a complimentary basis, such as a continental breakfast. Labor costs to provide these services should be charged to Salaries and Wages, if significant.

Contract Services. Contract Services includes any expenses associated with an activity that is normally charged to the department, but is now outsourced. Examples include the cost of contracting outside companies to wash windows, clean carpet and rugs, and exterminate and disinfect areas associated with the rooms department. The costs of maintaining the property management system are also included in Contract Services.

> ***Guest Relocation.*** This line item should be charged with the cost of renting accommodations in other properties when a decision is made to move a guest out of the property because of a lack of available rooms. This item should also include any incidental costs, gratuities, or compensation paid in connection with these circumstances.

> ***Guest Transportation.*** Guest transportation includes the cost of transporting guests to and from the property. If guest transportation costs are significant, a separate cost center may be established and transportation costs may be reported as suggested by Schedule 20.

> ***Laundry and Dry Cleaning.*** Laundry and Dry Cleaning includes the cost of contracting outside laundries for laundry and dry cleaning services applicable to the rooms department. These costs are determined from bills and invoices sent from outside laundries. Laundry and Dry Cleaning also includes the costs of dry cleaning curtains and draperies, and the costs of washing or cleaning awnings, carpets, and rugs in areas of the rooms department. For expenses applicable to the rooms department from the property's laundry facility, see House Laundry, Schedule 28.

> ***Linen.*** Linen includes the cost of towels, face cloths, bath mats, blankets, pillowcases, and sheets. Linen rental is also charged to this line item.

> ***Operating Supplies.*** Operating Supplies includes the cost of guest supplies, cleaning supplies, printing and stationery, and similar operating expenses applicable to the rooms department.

- *Guest Supplies.* Guest Supplies includes the cost of guestroom supplies and amenities that are provided on a gratis basis to the property's guests.

- *Cleaning Supplies.* Cleaning Supplies includes the cost of cleaning supplies applicable to the rooms department.

- *Printing and Stationery.* The cost of printed forms, service manuals, stationery, and office supplies, whether purchased from outside printers or produced internally, should be charged to this account when used by employees of the rooms department. Printing and stationery does not include the cost of writing materials supplied to guests. This expense is included under guest supplies. Printing and stationery also does not include the costs of supplies used by cashiers or for billing purposes. These expenses are not considered expenses of the rooms department. They are identified as undistributed operating expenses and are reported as Administrative and General Expenses on Schedule 15.

- *Other Operating Supplies.* Other Operating Supplies includes the costs of operating supplies applicable to the rooms department that do not apply to line items discussed previously.

Reservations. Reservations includes the cost of reservation service and central reservation system (including telecommunications expenses).

Telecommunications. Any telecommunications expenditures that can be directly related to the rooms department should be charged to this account.

Training. Training includes costs other than time associated with training employees. Examples include the costs of training materials, supplies, and instructor fees.

Uniforms. Uniforms includes the cost or rental of uniforms for employees of the rooms department. This expense item also includes costs of cleaning or repairing uniforms of rooms department employees.

Other. Expenses of the rooms department that do not apply to line items discussed previously are included in this line item.

Total Other Expenses

Total Other Expenses is calculated by adding all items listed under Other Expenses. The Total Other Expenses amount is the same amount that appears on the Summary Statement of Income in the Other Expenses column for Operated Departments—Rooms.

Total Expenses

Total Expenses is calculated by adding Total Payroll and Related Expenses to Total Other Expenses.

Departmental Income (Loss)

The income (or loss) of the rooms department is calculated by subtracting Total Expenses from Net Revenue. The Departmental Income (Loss) amount on Schedule 1 is the same amount that appears on the Summary Statement of Income in the Income (Loss) column for Operated Departments—Rooms.

FOOD

Food—Schedule 2

	Current Period
TOTAL REVENUE	$ _____
REVENUE	$
ALLOWANCES	_____
NET REVENUE	
COST OF SALES	
Cost of Food	
Less Cost of Employee Meals	
Less Food Transfers to Beverage	
Plus Beverage Transfers to Food	
Net Cost of Food	_____
Other Cost of Sales	_____
Total Cost of Sales	_____
GROSS PROFIT (LOSS) ON FOOD SALES	
OTHER INCOME	
Meeting Room Rentals	
Miscellaneous Banquet Income	
Service Charges	_____
Total Other Income	_____
GROSS PROFIT (LOSS) AND OTHER INCOME	
EXPENSES	
Salaries and Wages	
Employee Benefits	
Total Payroll and Related Expenses	_____
Other Expenses	
China, Glassware, Silver, and Linen	
Contract Services	
Laundry and Dry Cleaning	
Licenses	
Miscellaneous Banquet Expense	
Music and Entertainment	
Operating Supplies	
Telecommunications	
Training	
Uniforms	
Other	_____
Total Other Expenses	_____
TOTAL EXPENSES	_____
DEPARTMENTAL INCOME (LOSS)	$ _____

Many properties operate outlets that sell food. The Summary Statement of Income reports the Net Revenue, Cost of Sales, Payroll and Related Expenses, Other Expenses, and Income (Loss) of a property's food operations. These amounts appear on the Summary Statement of Income in columns across from the Food line item under Operated Departments. Amounts reported on the Summary Statement of Income should be supported by a supplemental schedule reflecting the results of food operations.

Food—Schedule 2 illustrates a format and identifies line items that commonly appear on a supplemental schedule for food operations. This format and the line items will vary according to the needs and requirements of individual properties. Therefore, the line items listed on the schedule may not apply to the food operation of every property. Individual properties should modify the schedule to meet their own needs and requirements.

Total Revenue

Total Revenue is the sum of Net Revenue and Total Other Income. The Total Revenue amount is the same amount that appears in the Net Revenues column of the Summary Statement of Income for Operated Departments—Food.

Revenue

Food Revenue includes revenue derived from food sales, including sales of coffee, tea, milk, and soft drinks. The revenue may be classified by outlet or the type of operation from which it is realized, such as restaurant, lounge, room service, banquets, and others. This line also includes revenue derived from other sources such as sales of candy and cigarettes sold in the various food facilities. When rooms and food are sold at an inclusive price, rooms revenue and food revenue should be separated and care should be taken to ensure that appropriate departments receive equitable revenue. (See Allocation of Packaged Revenues, page 35).

Allowances

Allowances includes rebates, refunds, and overcharges of revenue not known at the time of sale but adjusted at a later date.

Net Revenue

Net Revenue is calculated by subtracting Allowances from Revenue.

Cost of Sales

Cost of Food

The Cost of Food includes the cost of food served to guests and the cost of food items furnished for employee meals. Properties usually take a monthly food inventory. The Cost of Food is calculated by adding total food purchases to the value of the inventory at the beginning of the month and then subtracting the value of the inventory at the end of the month. Total food purchases are calculated by subtracting trade discounts (but *not* cash discounts) from the gross invoice price for all food items and then adding charges for transportation, delivery, and storage. If the policy of the property permits commissary and steward's sales, they should be credited to the Cost of Food when they are sold, at cost or a nominal mark-up. When the income on such sales is of sufficient importance to warrant it, the amount should be included in Food Revenue, and the cost of such sales charged to Cost of Food.

Cost of Employee Meals

Properties should calculate the Cost of Employee Meals either by an exact cost system, or, in cases where such a system is unwarranted, by a fixed price per meal. Regardless of the method used, the cost of furnishing meals for employees of the various departments within the property should be charged to those departments. These charges appear as an expense on appropriate departmental schedules under Payroll and Related Expenses—Employee Benefits.

Food Transfers to Beverage

Properties may transfer various food items to beverage department locations such as bars and lounges. These items typically fall into one of two groupings. The first group includes products used in drink preparation, such as oranges, lemons, olives, and celery. These items are charged to Cost of Beverage on the Schedule for the beverage department as a Food Transfer (see Beverage, Schedule 3). The second group of items transferred to beverage outlets includes snack foods, such as peanuts, pretzels, and popcorn, or other foods prepared in-house and sent to the beverage outlet for use on a complimentary basis as appetizers or hors d'oeuvres, typically during a happy hour. These items are charged to Other Expense—Gratis Food on the department schedule for the beverage department. (See Beverage, Schedule 3.)

Beverage Transfers to Food

Wine, brandy, and other alcoholic beverages are frequently used to flavor sauces, soups, and many entrées. They are also used to flame dishes in tableside cookery. Alcoholic beverages used for these purposes are included in calculating the Net Cost of Food as a transfer from beverage.

Net Cost of Food

The Net Cost of Food is calculated by subtracting the Cost of Employee Meals and Food Transfers to Beverage from Cost of Food and adding Beverage Transfers to Food.

Other Cost of Sales

This cost of sales item includes the costs associated with the sale of miscellaneous merchandise reported as revenue. Examples include the cost of candy and cigarettes.

Total Cost of Sales

The Total Cost of Sales is calculated by adding Net Cost of Food and Other Cost of Sales. The Total Cost of Sales appears in the Cost of Sales column on the Summary Statement of Income for Operated Departments—Food.

Gross Profit (Loss) on Food Sales

The Gross Profit (Loss) on Food Sales is calculated by subtracting Total Cost of Sales from Net Revenue.

Other Income

Other Income includes revenue from sources other than the sale of food. Detailed schedules for various food outlets may include under Other Income such revenue sources as meeting room rentals, miscellaneous banquet income, service charge, and others.

Meeting Room Rentals

Revenue derived from the rental of public meeting rooms, excluding guestrooms and suites, is included on this line.

Miscellaneous Banquet Income

Miscellaneous Banquet Income includes revenue derived from significant sales of merchandise or services in connection with banquet operations, such as the rental of audio/visual equipment.

Service Charges

Service Charges includes charges for services that are added to a customer's bill or banquet contract at either a fixed amount or a percentage of the sale.

Total Other Income

The Total Other Income amount is calculated by adding all of the amounts listed under Other Income.

Gross Profit (Loss) and Other Income

This amount is calculated by adding Gross Profit (Loss) on Food Sales to Total Other Income.

Expenses

Salaries and Wages

Salaries and Wages includes regular pay, overtime pay, vacation pay, sick pay, holiday pay, incentive pay, severance pay, banquet service charges, and bonuses for employees of the food department. This line item should also include any expense associated with leased labor, but not contract labor, which should be charged to Contract Services. If leased labor expense is significant, a separate line item called Leased Labor should be created and listed immediately after Salaries and Wages. For a classification of employees included in the food department, see Salaries and Wages, Schedule 29.

Employee Benefits

Employee Benefits includes payroll taxes, payroll-related insurance expense, pension, and other payroll-related expenses applicable to the food department. The cost of meals furnished to employees whose salaries and wages are charged to the food department is also included in this expense item. (See Payroll Taxes and Employee Benefits, Schedule 30.)

Total Payroll and Related Expenses

Total Payroll and Related Expenses is calculated by adding Salaries and Wages to Employee Benefits. The Total Payroll and Related Expenses amount is the same amount that appears on the Summary Statement of Income in the Payroll and Related Expenses column for Operated Departments—Food.

Other Expenses

This expense grouping includes significant food department expenses. Items appearing under Other Expenses vary from property to property. Examples of items that commonly appear as Other Expenses follow.

China, Glassware, Silver, and Linen. China, Glassware, Silver, and Linen includes the cost of the china, glassware, silver, or linen used in providing food service to the property's guests. Also included is the cost of rental linen services used by the food department. These expenses are usually accounted for in separate general ledger accounts.

Contract Services. Contract Services includes any expenses associated with an activity that is normally charged to the department, but is now outsourced. Examples include the cost of contracting outside companies to wash windows, degrease hoods, clean carpets and rugs and exterminate and disinfect areas of the food department. Contract Services also includes the cost of maintaining the point-of-sale system and equipment.

Laundry and Dry Cleaning. Laundry and Dry Cleaning includes the cost of contracting outside laundries for laundry and dry cleaning services applicable to the food department. These costs are determined from bills and invoices sent from outside laundries. Laundry and Dry Cleaning also includes the costs of dry cleaning curtains and draperies and the costs of washing or cleaning awnings associated with the food department. For expenses applicable to the food department from the property's laundry facility, see House Laundry, Schedule 28.

Licenses. Licenses includes the costs of all federal, state, and municipal licenses for the food facilities of the property, including music licenses.

Miscellaneous Banquet Expenses. Expenses associated with miscellaneous banquet income, such as the rental of audio/visual equipment, should be charged to this line item.

Music and Entertainment. Music and entertainment includes all costs associated with providing entertainment within the property's food facilities.

Operating Supplies. Operating Supplies includes the cost of cleaning supplies, guest supplies, menus, paper supplies, printing and stationery, utensils, and similar operating expenses applicable to the food department. If the cost of any of these items is significant, items and amounts should be listed separately from Operating Supplies.

- *Cleaning Supplies.* This item includes the costs associated with keeping food areas and equipment clean and sanitary.
- *Guest Supplies.* This item includes the cost of supplies and amenities that are provided on a gratis basis to guests of the property's food outlets.
- *Menus.* This item includes the costs associated with producing menus such as the cost of artwork, printing, and menu covers.
- *Paper Supplies.* This item includes the costs of paper supplies used by the food department.
- *Printing and Stationery.* The cost of printed forms, service manuals, stationery, and office supplies that are purchased from outside printers or produced internally should be charged to this account when they are used by employees of the food department.
- *Utensils.* This item includes the cost of all tools needed in the process of food preparation, such as butcher knives, spatulas, and whisks.
- *Other Operating Supplies.* This item includes costs of operating supplies applicable to the food department that do not apply to line items discussed previously.

Telecommunications. Any telecommunication expenditures that can be directly related to the food department should be charged to this account.

Training. Training includes costs other than time associated with training employees. Examples include the costs of training materials, supplies, and instructor fees.

Uniforms. Uniforms includes the cost or rental of uniforms for employees of the food department. This item also includes costs of cleaning or repairing uniforms of food department employees.

Other. Expenses of the food department that do not apply to line items discussed previously are included in this line item.

Total Other Expenses

Total Other Expenses is calculated by adding all items listed under Other Expenses. The Total Other Expenses amount on Schedule 2 is the same amount that appears on the Summary Statement of Income in the Other Expenses column for Operated Departments—Food.

Total Expenses

Total Expenses is calculated by adding Total Payroll and Related Expenses to Total Other Expenses.

Departmental Income (Loss)

The income (or loss) of the food department is calculated by subtracting Total Expenses from the amount shown as Gross Profit and Other Income. The Departmental Income (Loss) amount on Schedule 2 is the same amount that appears on the

Summary Statement of Income in the Income (Loss) column for Operated Departments—Food.

BEVERAGE

Beverage—Schedule 3

	Current Period
TOTAL REVENUE	$ _____
REVENUE	$
ALLOWANCES	_____
NET REVENUE	
COST OF SALES	
Cost of Beverage	
Less Beverage Transfers to Food	
Plus Food Transfers to Beverage	_____
Net Cost of Beverage	
Other Cost of Sales	_____
Total Cost of Sales	_____
GROSS PROFIT (LOSS) ON BEVERAGE SALES	
OTHER INCOME	
Cover Charges	
Service Charges	_____
Total Other Income	_____
GROSS PROFIT (LOSS) AND OTHER INCOME	
EXPENSES	
Salaries and Wages	
Employee Benefits	_____
Total Payroll and Related Expenses	_____
Other Expenses	
China, Glassware, Silver, and Linen	
Contract Services	
Gratis Food	
Laundry and Dry Cleaning	
Licenses	
Music and Entertainment	
Operating Supplies	
Telecommunications	
Training	
Uniforms	
Other	_____
Total Other Expenses	_____
TOTAL EXPENSES	_____
DEPARTMENTAL INCOME (LOSS)	$ _____

Many properties operate outlets that sell beverage items. The Summary Statement of Income reports the Net Revenue, Cost of Sales, Payroll and Related Expenses, Other Expenses, and Income (Loss) of a property's beverage operations. These amounts appear on the Summary Statement of Income in columns across from the Beverage line item under Operated Departments. Amounts reported on the Summary Statement of Income should be supported by a supplemental schedule reflecting the results of beverage operations.

Beverage—Schedule 3 illustrates a format and identifies line items that commonly appear on a supplemental schedule for beverage operations. This format and the line items will vary according to the needs and requirements of individual properties. Therefore, the line items listed on the schedule may not apply to the beverage operation of every property. Individual properties should modify the schedule to meet their own needs and requirements.

Total Revenue

Total Revenue is the sum of Net Revenue and Total Other Income. The Total Revenue amount is the same amount that appears in the Net Revenues column of the Summary Statement of Income for Operated Departments—Beverage.

Revenue

Beverage Revenue includes revenue derived from alcoholic beverage sales and soft drinks. Beverage revenue may be classified by outlet or the type of operation from which it is realized, such as restaurant, lounge, room service, banquets, mini-bars, and others. Revenue may also be classified by type of beverage, such as wine, liquor, beer and ale, and others. This line also includes revenue derived from other sources such as sales of snacks and cigarettes sold in the various beverage facilities.

Allowances

Allowances includes rebates, refunds, and overcharges of revenue not known at the time of sale but adjusted at a later date.

Net Revenue

Net revenue is calculated by subtracting Allowances from Revenue.

Cost of Sales

Cost of Beverage

The Cost of Beverage includes the cost of wines, liquors, beers and ales, and other items such as mineral waters, fruits, syrups, sugar, and bitters that are served as beverages or used in the preparation of mixed drinks. Properties usually take a monthly beverage inventory. The Cost of Beverage is calculated by adding total beverage purchases to the value of the inventory at the beginning of the month and by subtracting trade discounts (but *not* cash discounts) from the gross invoice price for all beverage items and then adding import duties; charges for transportation, delivery, and storage; and taxes based on the quantity and alcoholic content of beverage items purchased or consumed. Deposit refunds and sales of empty bottles, barrels, or other items previously charged as a cost should be credited to Cost of Beverage.

Beverage Transfers to Food

Wine, brandy, and other alcoholic beverages are frequently used to flavor sauces, soups, and many entrées. They are also used to flame dishes in tableside cookery. The cost of beverages used for these purposes should be subtracted from the Cost of Beverage and added to the Cost of Food (see Food, Schedule 2).

Food Transfers to Beverage

Properties may transfer various food products to bar outlets for use in drink preparation, such as oranges, lemons, olives, and celery. These items should be included in calculating the Net Cost of Beverage.

Net Cost of Beverage

The Net Cost of Beverage is calculated by subtracting Beverage Transfers to Food from the Cost of Beverage and adding Food Transfers to Beverage.

Other Cost of Sales

This cost of sales item includes the costs associated with the sale of merchandise reported as revenue. Examples include the cost of snacks and cigarettes.

Total Cost of Sales

The Total Cost of Sales is calculated by adding Net Cost of Beverage and Other Cost of Sales. The Total Cost of Sales appears in the Cost of Sales column on the Summary Statement of Income for Operated Departments—Beverage.

Gross Profit (Loss) on Beverage Sales

The Gross Profit (Loss) on Beverage Sales is calculated by subtracting Total Cost of Sales from Net Revenue.

Other Income

Other Income includes revenue from sources other than the sale of beverages. Detailed schedules for various beverage outlets may include under Other Income such revenue sources as Cover Charges and Service Charges.

Cover Charges

Cover Charges includes revenue derived from charging a specific rate per person, which is intended to defray such expenses as music and entertainment.

Service Charges

Service Charges includes charges for services that are added to a customer's bill or banquet contract at either a fixed amount or a percentage of the sale.

Total Other Income

The Total Other Income amount is calculated by adding all of the amounts listed under Other Income.

Gross Profit (Loss) and Other Income

This amount is calculated by adding Gross Profit (Loss) on Beverage Sales to Total Other Income.

Expenses

Salaries and Wages

Salaries and Wages includes regular pay, overtime pay, vacation pay, sick pay, holiday pay, incentive pay, severance pay, banquet service charges, and bonuses for employees of the beverage department. This line item should also include any expense associated with leased labor, but not contract labor, which should be charged to Contract Services. If leased labor expense is significant, a separate line item called Leased Labor should be created and listed immediately after Salaries and Wages. For a classification of employees included in the beverage department, see Salaries and Wages, Schedule 29.

Employee Benefits

Employee Benefits includes payroll taxes, payroll-related insurance expense, pension, and other payroll-related expenses applicable to the beverage department. The cost of meals furnished to employees whose salaries and wages are charged to the beverage department is also included in this expense item. (See Payroll Taxes and Employee Benefits, Schedule 30.)

Total Payroll and Related Expenses

Total Payroll and Related Expenses is calculated by adding Salaries and Wages to Employee Benefits. The Total Payroll and Related Expenses amount is the same amount that appears on the Summary Statement of Income in the Payroll and Related Expenses column for Operated Department—Beverage.

Other Expenses

This expense grouping includes significant beverage department expenses. Items appearing under Other Expenses vary from property to property. Examples of items that commonly appear as Other Expenses follow.

China, Glassware, Silver, and Linen. China, Glassware, Silver, and Linen includes the cost of the china, glassware, silver, or linen used in providing beverage service to the property's guests. Also included is the cost of rental linen services used by the beverage department. These expenses are usually accounted for in separate general ledger accounts.

Contract Services. Contract Services includes any expenses associated with an activity that is normally charged to the department, but is now outsourced. Examples include the cost of contracting outside companies to wash windows, clean carpets and rugs, and exterminate and disinfect areas of the beverage department. Contract Services also includes the cost of maintaining the point-of-sale and beverage dispensing systems.

Gratis Food. Properties may offer snack foods, such as peanuts, pretzels, and popcorn or other foods prepared in-house on a complimentary basis as appetizers or hors d'oeuvres in beverage outlets, typically during a happy hour. The cost of these items is charged to the Gratis Food line.

Laundry and Dry Cleaning. Laundry and Dry Cleaning includes the cost of contracting outside laundries for laundry and dry cleaning services applicable to the beverage department. These costs are determined from bills and invoices sent from outside laundries. Laundry and Dry Cleaning also includes the costs of dry cleaning curtains and draperies and the costs of washing or cleaning awnings associated with the beverage department. For expenses applicable to the beverage department from the property's laundry facility, see House Laundry, Schedule 28.

Licenses. Licenses includes the costs of all federal, state, and municipal licenses for the beverage facilities of the property, including music licenses.

Music and Entertainment. Music and Entertainment includes all costs associated with providing entertainment within the property's beverage facilities.

Operating Supplies. Operating Supplies includes the cost of cleaning supplies, guest supplies, menus, paper supplies, printing and stationery, and similar operating expenses applicable to the beverage department. If the cost of any of these items is significant, items and amounts should be listed separately from Operating Supplies.

- *Cleaning Supplies.* This item includes the costs associated with keeping beverage areas and equipment clean and sanitary.

- *Guest Supplies.* This item includes the cost of supplies and amenities that are provided on a gratis basis to guests of the property's beverage outlets.

- *Menus.* This item includes the costs associated with producing menus such as the cost of artwork, printing, and menu covers.

- *Paper Supplies.* This item includes the costs of paper supplies used by the beverage department.

- *Printing and Stationery.* The cost of printed forms, service manuals, stationery and office supplies that are purchased from outside printers or produced internally should be charged to this account when they are used by employees of the beverage department.

- *Other Operating Supplies.* This item includes costs of operating supplies applicable to the beverage department that do not apply to line items discussed previously.

Telecommunications. Any telecommunication expenditures that can be directly related to the beverage department should be charged to this account.

Training. Training includes costs other than time associated with training employees. Examples include the costs of training materials, supplies, and instructor fees.

Uniforms. Uniforms includes the cost or rental of uniforms for employees of the beverage department. This item also includes costs of cleaning or repairing uniforms of beverage department employees.

Other. Expenses of the beverage department that do not apply to line items discussed previously are included in this line item.

Total Other Expenses

Total Other Expenses is calculated by adding all items listed under Other Expenses. The Total Other Expenses amount on Schedule 3 is the same amount that appears on the Summary Statement of Income in the Other Expenses column for Operated Departments—Beverage.

Total Expenses

Total Expenses is calculated by adding Total Payroll and Related Expenses to Total Other Expenses.

Departmental Income (Loss)

The income (or loss) of the beverage department is calculated by subtracting Total Expenses from the amount shown as Gross Profit (Loss) and Other Income. The Departmental Income (Loss) amount on Schedule 3 is the same amount that appears on the Summary Statement of Income in the Income (Loss) column for Operated Departments—Beverage.

TELECOMMUNICATIONS

Telecommunications—Schedule 4

	Current Period
REVENUE	$
ALLOWANCES	————
NET REVENUE	
COST OF CALLS	
Long-Distance	
Local	
Utility Tax	
Other	————
Total Cost of Calls	
GROSS PROFIT (LOSS)	
EXPENSES	
Salaries and Wages	
Employee Benefits	————
Total Payroll and Related Expenses	————
Other Expenses	
Contract Services	
Printing and Stationery	
Telecommunications	
Training	
Other	————
Total Other Expenses	————
TOTAL EXPENSES	————
DEPARTMENTAL INCOME (LOSS)	$ ═══

Telecommunications—Schedule 4 illustrates a format and identifies line items that commonly appear on a supplemental schedule supporting the Net Revenue, Cost of Sales, Payroll and Related Expenses, Other Expenses, and Income (Loss) amounts reported on the Summary Statement of Income for Operated Departments—Telecommunications. This format and the line items will vary according to the needs and requirements of individual properties. Therefore, the line items listed on the schedule may not apply to the telecommunication operations of every property. Individual properties should modify the schedule to meet their own needs and requirements.

Revenue

This account should be credited with revenue derived from the use of telecommunication facilities by guests, divided into local calls, long-distance calls, service charges, commissions received from non-owned pay stations, and revenue from owned pay stations. If the property uses several service providers, it may identify revenue attributable to each provider. In addition, this account should include revenue derived from guests using facsimile services, modem services,and other telecommunication services when the cost of calls for such services is included in the telecommunications department. The account should not be credited with any amounts for telecommunication services used by management or other departments of the property.

Allowances

Allowances includes rebates, refunds, and overcharges of revenue not known at the time of sale but adjusted at a later date.

Net Revenue

Net Revenue is calculated by subtracting Allowances from Revenue. The Net Revenue amount is the same amount that appears on the Summary Statement of Income in the Net Revenues column for Operated Departments—Telecommunications.

Cost of Calls

The total of the amounts billed by the telecommunication companies for long-distance and local calls through the switchboard constitutes the gross cost of calls. If the property chooses to separate the revenue by service provider, the Cost of Calls should also be separated by provider. All administrative calls, if material, should be charged to the appropriate departments. Utility taxes related to the revenue generated from resale of telecommunication services should also be charged to this department.

The cost of automatic internal communicating systems should not be charged to this account but included in the account provided under Administrative and General Expenses.

The Cost of Calls amount is the same amount that appears on the Summary Statement of Income in the Cost of Sales column for Operated Departments—Telecommunications.

Gross Profit (Loss)

The Gross Profit (Loss) is calculated by subtracting the Cost of Calls from Net Revenue.

Expenses

Salaries and Wages

Salaries and Wages includes regular pay, overtime pay, vacation pay, sick pay, holiday pay, incentive pay, severance pay, and bonuses for employees of the telecommunications department. This line item should also include any expense associated with leased labor, but not contract labor, which should be charged to Contract Services. If leased labor expense is significant, a separate line item called Leased Labor should be created and listed immediately after Salaries and Wages. For a classification of employees included in the telecommunications department, see Salaries and Wages, Schedule 29.

Employee Benefits

Employee Benefits includes payroll taxes, payroll-related insurance expense, pension, and other payroll-related expenses applicable to the telecommunications department. The cost of meals furnished to employees whose salaries and wages are charged to the telecommunications department is also included in this expense item. (See Payroll Taxes and Employee Benefits, Schedule 30.)

Total Payroll and Related Expenses

Total Payroll and Related Expenses is calculated by adding Salaries and Wages to Employee Benefits. The Total Payroll and Related Expenses amount is the same amount that appears on the Summary Statement of Income in the Payroll and Related Expenses column for Operated Departments—Telecommunications.

Other Expenses

This expense grouping includes significant telecommunications department expenses. Items appearing under Other Expenses vary from property to property. Examples of items which commonly appear as Other Expenses follow.

Contract Services. Contract Services includes any expense associated with an activity that is normally charged to the department, but is now outsourced. Examples include equipment maintenance and service contracts related to the telecommunications department.

Printing and Stationery. The cost of printed forms, service manuals, traffic sheets, telecommunication vouchers, message envelopes, stationery and office supplies, whether purchased from outside printers or produced internally, should be charged to this account when used by employees of the telecommunications department.

Telecommunications. Any telecommunication expenditures that can be directly related to the telecommunications department should be charged to this account.

Training. Training includes costs other than time associated with training employees. Examples include the costs of training materials, supplies, and instructor fees.

Other. Items such as telephone directory covers and holders and the cost of out-of-town directories not included under other captions should be grouped under this caption. If these costs are departmentally identifiable and significant, they should be charged to the department or cost center.

Total Other Expenses

Total Other Expenses is calculated by adding all items listed under Other Expenses. The Total Other Expenses amount on Schedule 4 is the same amount that appears on the Summary Statement of Income in the Other Expenses column for Operated Departments—Telecommunications.

Total Expenses

Total Expenses is calculated by adding Total Payroll and Related Expenses to Total Other Expenses.

Departmental Income (Loss)

The income (or loss) of the telecommunications department is calculated by subtracting Total Expenses from Gross Profit (Loss). The Departmental Income (Loss) amount on Schedule 4 is the same amount that appears on the Summary Statement of Income in the Income (Loss) column for Operated Departments—Telecommunications.

GARAGE AND PARKING

Garage and Parking—Schedule 5

	Current Period
REVENUE	$
ALLOWANCES	_____
NET REVENUE	
COST OF MERCHANDISE SOLD	_____
GROSS PROFIT (LOSS)	
EXPENSES	
Salaries and Wages	
Employee Benefits	
Total Payroll and Related Expenses	_____
Other Expenses	_____
Contract Services	
Licenses	
Management Fee	
Operating Supplies	
Telecommunications	
Training	
Uniforms	
Other	_____
Total Other Expenses	_____
TOTAL EXPENSES	_____
DEPARTMENTAL INCOME (LOSS)	$ _____

Garage and Parking—Schedule 5 illustrates a format and identifies line items that commonly appear on a supplemental schedule supporting the Net Revenue, Cost of Sales, Payroll and Related Expenses, Other Expenses, and Income (Loss) amounts reported on the Summary Statement of Income for Operated Departments—Garage and Parking. This format and the line items will vary according to the needs and requirements of individual properties. Therefore, the line items listed on Schedule 5 may not apply to the garage and parking operations of every property. Individual properties should modify Schedule 5 to meet their own needs and requirements.

Revenue

Garage and parking Revenue includes revenue derived from parking and storage, merchandise, and other services. Parking and storage includes fees received for parking services rendered. Merchandise includes sales of merchandise such as gas, oil, windshield wipers, and other items.

Properties may classify the items appearing under Revenue according to their individual needs and requirements. If, in relation to the total revenue generated by the garage and parking operation, a significant amount of revenue is generated by the sale of an item or by a group of similar items, the item or category of items should be detailed separately.

Allowances

Allowances includes rebates, refunds, and overcharges of revenue not known at the time of sale but adjusted at a later date.

Net Revenue

Net Revenue is calculated by subtracting Allowances from Revenue. The Net Revenue amount is the same amount that appears on the Summary Statement of Income in the Net Revenues column for Operated Departments—Garage and Parking.

Cost of Merchandise Sold

The Cost of Merchandise Sold for the garage and parking operation is calculated by adding total merchandise purchases to the value of inventory at the beginning of the period and then subtracting the value of inventory at the end of the period. Total merchandise is calculated by subtracting trade discounts (but *not* cash discounts) from the purchase price of merchandise and then adding transportation and delivery charges.

If individual merchandise items or categories of similar items are listed separately under Revenue, these same items or categories of items should also be listed separately under Cost of Merchandise Sold.

The Cost of Merchandise Sold amount is the same amount that appears on the Summary Statement of Income in the Cost of Sales column for Operated Departments—Garage and Parking.

Gross Profit (Loss)

The Gross Profit (Loss) amount is calculated by subtracting Cost of Merchandise Sold from Net Revenue.

Expenses

Salaries and Wages

Salaries and Wages includes regular pay, overtime pay, vacation pay, sick pay, holiday pay, incentive pay, severance pay, and bonuses for garage and parking employees. This line item should also include any expense associated with leased labor, but not contract labor, which should be charged to Contract Services. If leased labor expense is significant, a separate line item called Leased Labor should be created and listed immediately after Salaries and Wages. For a classification of employees included in the garage and parking department, see Salaries and Wages, Schedule 29.

Employee Benefits

Employee Benefits includes payroll taxes, payroll-related insurance expense, pension, and other related expenses applicable to the garage and parking operation. The cost of meals furnished to employees whose salaries and wages are charged to the garage and parking department is also included in this expense item. (See Payroll Taxes and Employee Benefits, Schedule 30.)

Total Payroll and Related Expenses

Total Payroll and Related Expenses is calculated by adding Salaries and Wages to Employee Benefits. The Total Payroll and Related Expenses amount is the same amount that appears on the Summary Statement of Income in the Payroll and Related Expenses column for Operated Departments—Garage and Parking.

Other Expenses

This expense grouping includes significant expenses of garage and parking operations. Items appearing under Other Expenses vary from property to property. Examples of items that commonly appear as Other Expenses follow.

Contract Services. Contract Services includes any expense associated with an activity that is normally charged to the department, but is now outsourced. Examples include using vendors to clean the garage and stripe parking lanes, hiring an outside parking company to manage the parking lots, and hiring contract labor as mechanics for auto repair.

Licenses. Licenses includes the costs of all licenses and permits that are necessary for the garage and parking operation.

Management Fee. Management Fee includes the amount paid to professional garage operators for the management of the property's garage operation.

Operating Supplies. Operating Supplies includes costs of items such as gas, oil, and parts that are used in the garage and parking operation and that are not chargeable to customers.

Telecommunications. Any telecommunication expenditures that can be directly related to the garage and parking department should be charged to this account.

Training. Training includes costs other than time associated with training employees. Examples include the costs of training materials, supplies, and instructor fees.

Uniforms. Uniforms includes the cost or rental of uniforms for garage and parking employees. This expense item also includes costs of cleaning or repairing uniforms of garage and parking employees.

Other. Expenses of the garage and parking department that do not apply to line items discussed previously are included in this line item. If the expenses for individual items or categories of similar items are significant in amount, they should be listed separately.

Total Other Expenses

Total Other Expenses is calculated by adding all items listed under Other Expenses. The Total Other Expenses amount is the same amount that appears on the

Summary Statement of Income in the Other Expenses column for Operated Departments—Garage and Parking.

Total Expenses

Total Expenses is calculated by adding Total Payroll and Related Expenses to Total Other Expenses.

Departmental Income (Loss)

The income (or loss) from garage and parking operations is calculated by subtracting Total Expenses from Gross Profit (Loss). The Departmental Income (Loss) amount on Schedule 5 is the same amount that appears on the Summary Statement of Income in the Income (Loss) column for Operated Departments—Garage and Parking.

GOLF COURSE

Golf Course—Schedule 6

	Current Period
REVENUE	$
ALLOWANCES	_____
NET REVENUE	
EXPENSES, EXCLUDING COURSE MAINTENANCE	
Salaries and Wages	
Employee Benefits	_____
Total Payroll and Related Expenses	_____
Other Expenses	
Contract Services	
Gasoline and Lubricants	
Golf Car Batteries/Electricity	
Golf Car Repairs and Maintenance	
Laundry and Dry Cleaning	
Operating Supplies	
Professional Services	
Telecommunications	
Tournament Expenses	
Training	
Other	_____
Total Other Expenses	_____
TOTAL EXPENSES EXCLUDING COURSE MAINTENANCE	_____
COURSE MAINTENANCE EXPENSES	
Salaries and Wages	
Employee Benefits	_____
Total Payroll and Related Expenses	_____
Other Expenses	
Contract Services	
Fertilizers, Insecticides, and Topsoil	
Gasoline and Lubricants	
Repairs and Maintenance	
General	
Irrigation	
Machinery and Equipment	
Refuse Removal	
Sand and Top Dressing	
Seeds, Flowers, and Shrubs	
Telecommunications	
Training	
Uniforms	
Water	
Other	_____
Total Other Expenses	_____
TOTAL COURSE MAINTENANCE EXPENSES	_____
TOTAL GOLF COURSE EXPENSES	_____
DEPARTMENTAL INCOME (LOSS)	$ _____

Golf Course—Schedule 6 illustrates a format and identifies line items which commonly appear on a supplemental schedule supporting the Net Revenue, Payroll and Related Expenses, Other Expenses, and Income (Loss) amounts reported on the Summary Statement of Income for Operated Departments—Golf Course. This format and the line items will vary according to the needs and requirements of individual properties. Therefore, the line items listed on Schedule 6 may not apply to the operations of every property. Individual properties should modify Schedule 6 to meet their own needs and requirements.

Revenue

Golf course Revenue includes revenue derived from driving and practice range fees, golf car rentals, golf club rentals, greens fees, annual and season passes and punch cards, guest privilege fees, membership fees, tournament fees, and other, such as storage costs and golf club cleaning and repair. Separate categories should be used to identify significant revenue items.

Allowances

Allowances includes rebates, refunds, and overcharges of revenue not known at the time of sale but adjusted at a later date.

Net Revenue

Net Revenue is calculated by subtracting Allowances from Revenue. The Net Revenue amount is the same amount that appears on the Summary Statement of Income in the Net Revenues column for Operated Departments—Golf Course.

Expenses, Excluding Course Maintenance

Salaries and Wages

Salaries and Wages includes regular pay, overtime pay, vacation pay, sick pay, holiday pay, incentive pay, severance pay, and bonuses for non-maintenance employees of the golf course. This line item should also include any expense associated with leased labor, but not contract labor, which should be charged to Contract Services. If leased labor expense is significant, a separate line item called Leased Labor should be created and listed immediately after Salaries and Wages. For a classification of employees included in the golf course department, see Salaries and Wages, Schedule 29.

Employee Benefits

Employee Benefits includes payroll taxes, payroll-related insurance expense, pension, and other payroll-related expenses applicable to the golf course. The cost of meals furnished to employees whose salaries and wages are charged to the golf course is also included in this expense item. (See Payroll Taxes and Employee Benefits, Schedule 30.)

Total Payroll and Related Expenses

Total Payroll and Related Expenses is calculated by adding Salaries and Wages to Employee Benefits. The Total Payroll and Related Expenses amount is added to the

Total Payroll and Related Expenses for course maintenance (described below) and the sum is the amount that appears on the Summary Statement of Income in the Payroll and Related Expenses column for Operated Departments—Golf Course.

Other Expenses

This expense grouping includes significant golf course expenses. Items appearing under Other Expenses vary from property to property. Examples of items that commonly appear as Other Expenses follow.

Contract Services. Contract services include any expenses associated with an activity that is normally charged to the department, but is now outsourced. Examples include equipment maintenance and service contracts related to the golf course department.

Gasoline and Lubricants. The cost of gasoline and lubricants for gas powered golf cars is charged to this item.

Golf Car Batteries/Electricity. The cost of batteries and the costs associated with charging the batteries should be charged to this account.

Golf Car Repairs and Maintenance. The cost of repairs and maintenance of golf cars should be charged to this account.

Laundry and Dry Cleaning. Laundry and Dry Cleaning includes the cost of contracting outside laundries for services applicable to the operation of the golf course. These costs are determined from bills and invoices sent from outside laundries. For expenses applicable to the golf course from the property's laundry facility, see House Laundry, Schedule 28.

Operating Supplies. The cost of supplies used in the operation of the golf course should be charged to this account.

Professional Services. The cost of contract professionals engaged to assist management in golf course operations, tournaments, and promotions should be charged to this account.

Telecommunications. Any telecommunications expenditures that can be directly related to the golf course should be charged to this account.

Tournament Expenses. All expenses incurred in administering golf tournaments should be charged to this account.

Training. Training includes costs other than time associated with training employees. Examples include the costs of training materials, supplies, and instructor fees.

Other. Expenses of the golf course department that do not apply to line items discussed previously are included in this line item.

Total Other Expenses

Total Other Expenses is calculated by adding all items listed under Other Expenses. The Total Other Expenses amount is added to Total Other Expenses for course maintenance (described below) and the sum is the amount that appears on the Summary Statement of Income in the Other Expenses column for Operated Departments—Golf Course.

Total Expenses Excluding Course Maintenance

Total Expenses is calculated by adding Total Payroll and Related Expenses to Total Other Expenses.

Course Maintenance Expenses

Salaries and Wages

Salaries and Wages includes regular pay, overtime pay, sick pay, holiday pay, incentive pay, severance pay, and bonuses for employees responsible for the maintenance of the golf course. This line item should also include any expense associated with leased labor, but not contract labor, which should be charged to Contract Services. If leased labor expense is significant, a separate line item called Leased Labor should be created and listed immediately after Salaries and Wages. For a classification of employees included in course maintenance, see Salaries and Wages, Schedule 29.

Employee Benefits

Employee Benefits includes payroll taxes, payroll-related insurance expense, pension, and other payroll-related expenses applicable to employees responsible for the maintenance of the golf course. The cost of meals furnished to employees whose salaries and wages are charged to golf course maintenance is also included in this expense item. (See Payroll Taxes and Employee Benefits, Schedule 30.)

Total Payroll and Related Expenses

Total Payroll and Related Expenses is calculated by adding Salaries and Wages to Employee Benefits. The Total Payroll and Related Expenses amount for employees responsible for the maintenance of the golf course is added to the Total Payroll and Related Expenses for other golf course employees and the sum is the amount that appears on the Summary Statement of Income in the Payroll and Related Expenses column for Operated Departments—Golf Course.

Other Expenses

This expense grouping includes significant golf course maintenance expenses. Items appearing under Other Expenses vary from property to property. Examples of items that commonly appear as Other Expenses follow.

Contract Services. Contract Services includes any expenses associated with an activity that is normally charged to the department, but is now outsourced. Examples include the cost of course maintenance and service contracts related to maintenance of the golf course.

Fertilizers, Insecticides, and Topsoil. The cost of these items should be charged to this account.

Gasoline and Lubricants. The cost of gasoline and lubricants for mowers, tractors and trucks used on the golf course should be charged to this item.

Repairs and Maintenance—General. All costs incurred in keeping course facilities such as buildings, fences, bridges, roads, and paths in proper physical condition should be charged to this account.

Repairs and Maintenance—Irrigation. The cost of repairing golf course water and drainage systems, sprinklers, water controllers, and computerized water systems should be charged to this account.

Repairs and Maintenance—Machinery and Equipment. The cost of repairing golf course equipment such as mowers, tractors, trucks, and water and drainage systems should be charged to this account.

Refuse Removal. Refuse Removal includes all costs associated with removing refuse from the golf course.

Sand and Top Dressing. The cost of sand and top dressing used on the golf course should be charged to this account.

Seeds, Flowers, and Shrubs. The cost of seeds, flowers, and shrubs used on the golf course should be charged to this account.

Telecommunications. Any telecommunications expenditures that can be directly related to golf club maintenance should be charged to this account.

Training. Training includes costs other than time associated with training employees. Examples include the costs of training materials, supplies, and instructor fees.

Uniforms. Uniforms includes the cost or rental of uniforms for employees whose salaries and wages are charged to golf course maintenance. This item also includes the costs of cleaning or repairing uniforms for these employees, as well as other related costs.

Water. The cost of water and irrigation used on the golf course should be charged to this account.

Other. Expenses of golf course maintenance that do not apply to line items discussed previously are included in this line item.

Total Other Expenses

Total Other Expenses is calculated by adding all items listed under Other Expenses for course maintenance.

Total Course Maintenance Expenses

This total is calculated by adding Total Payroll and Related Expenses and Total Other Expenses. Total Course Maintenance Expenses is added to Total Expenses

Excluding Course Maintenance and the sum is the amount that appears on the Statement of Income in the Other Expenses column for Operated Departments—Golf Course.

Total Golf Course Expenses

Total Golf Course Expenses is calculated by adding Total Expenses Excluding Course Maintenance and Total Course Maintenance Expenses.

Departmental Income (Loss)

The income (or loss) of the golf course is calculated by subtracting Total Golf Course Expenses from Net Revenue. The Departmental Income (Loss) amount on Schedule 6 is the same amount that appears on the Summary Statement of Income in the Income (Loss) column for Operated Departments—Golf Course.

GOLF PRO SHOP

Golf Pro Shop—Schedule 7	Current Period
TOTAL REVENUE	$ _____
REVENUE	$ _____
ALLOWANCES	
NET REVENUE	
COST OF MERCHANDISE SOLD	_____
GROSS PROFIT (LOSS)	
OTHER INCOME	
GROSS PROFIT (LOSS) AND OTHER INCOME	
EXPENSES	
Salaries and Wages	
Employee Benefits	_____
Total Payroll and Related Expenses	_____
Other Expenses	
Contract Services	
Operating Supplies	
Telecommunications	
Training	
Other	_____
Total Other Expenses	_____
TOTAL EXPENSES	_____
DEPARTMENTAL INCOME (LOSS)	$ _____

Golf Pro Shop—Schedule 7 illustrates a format and identifies line items that commonly appear on a supplemental schedule supporting the Net Revenue, Cost of Sales, Payroll and Related Expenses, Other Expenses, and Income (Loss) amounts reported on the Summary Statement of Income for Operated Departments—Golf Pro Shop. This format and the line items will vary according to the needs and requirements of individual properties. Therefore, the line items listed on Schedule 7 may not apply to the operations of every property. Individual properties should modify Schedule 7 to meet their own needs and requirements.

Total Revenue

Total Revenue is the sum of Net Revenue and Other Income. The Total Revenue amount is the same amount that appears on the Summary Statement of Income in the Net Revenues column for Operated Departments—Golf Pro Shop.

Revenue

Revenue for the golf pro shop includes all revenue derived from sales of accessories, golf apparel, golf balls, and golf clubs. Separate categories should be used to identify significant revenue items.

Allowances

Allowances includes rebates, refunds, and overcharges of revenue not known at the time of sale but adjusted at a later date.

Net Revenue

Net Revenue is calculated by subtracting Allowances from Revenue.

Cost of Merchandise Sold

Properties usually take a monthly inventory of pro shop merchandise. The Cost of Merchandise Sold is calculated by adding total pro shop merchandise purchases to the value of inventory at the beginning of the month and then subtracting the value of inventory at the end of the month. Total pro shop merchandise purchases is calculated by subtracting trade discounts (but *not* cash discounts) from the purchase price of the merchandise and then adding transportation and delivery charges. If separate categories were used to identify significant Revenue items, these same categories should be used to list the related Cost of Merchandise Sold. The cost of merchandise Sold is the same amount that appears on the Summary Statement of Income in the Cost of Sales column for Operated Departments—Golf Pro Shop.

Gross Profit (Loss)

The Gross Profit (Loss) amount is calculated by subtracting Cost of Merchandise Sold from Net Revenue.

Other Income

This account should be credited with revenue from other sources such as the cleaning and repairing of golf clubs and accessories.

Expenses

Salaries and Wages

Salaries and Wages includes regular pay, overtime pay, vacation pay, sick pay, holiday pay, incentive pay, severance pay, and bonuses for employees of the golf pro shop. All commissions paid to the golf pro or other employees of this department should be charged to this account. This line item should also include any expense associated with leased labor, but not contract labor, which should be charged to Contract Services. If leased labor expense is significant, a separate line item called Leased Labor should be created and listed immediately after Salaries and Wages. For a classification of employees included in the golf pro shop, see Salaries and Wages, Schedule 29.

Employee Benefits

Employee Benefits includes payroll taxes, payroll-related insurance expense, pension, and other payroll-related expenses applicable to the golf pro shop. The cost of meals furnished to employees whose salaries and wages are charged to the golf pro shop is also included in this expense item. (See Payroll Taxes and Employee Benefits, Schedule 30.)

Total Payroll and Related Expenses

Total Payroll and Related Expenses is calculated by adding Salaries and Wages to Employee Benefits. The Total Payroll and Related Expenses amount is the same amount that appears on the Summary Statement of Income in the Payroll and Related Expenses column for Operated Departments—Golf Pro Shop.

Other Expenses

This expense grouping includes significant golf pro shop expenses. Items appearing under Other Expenses vary from property to property. Examples of items that commonly appear as Other Expenses follow.

Contract Services. Contract Services includes any expense associated with an activity that is normally charged to the department but is now outsourced. Examples include the cost of equipment maintenance and service contracts related to the golf pro shop.

Operating Supplies. The cost of any supplies used in the golf pro shop should be charged to this account.

Telecommunications. Any telecommunications expenditures that can be directly related to the golf pro shop should be charged to this account.

Training. Training includes costs other than time associated with training employees. Examples include the costs of training materials, supplies, and instructor fees.

Other. Expenses of the golf pro shop that do not apply to the line items discussed previously are included in this line item.

Total Other Expenses

Total Other Expenses is calculated by adding all items listed under Other Expenses. The Total Other Expenses amount is the same amount that appears on the Summary Statement of Income in the Other Expenses column for Operated Departments—Golf Pro Shop.

Total Expenses

Total Expenses is calculated by adding Total Payroll and Related Expenses to Total Other Expenses.

Departmental Income (Loss)

The income (or loss) of the golf pro shop is calculated by subtracting Total Expenses from the sum of Gross Profit (Loss) and Other Income. The Departmental Income (Loss) amount on Schedule 7 is the same amount that appears on the Summary Statement of Income in the Income (Loss) column for Operated Departments—Golf Pro Shop.

GUEST LAUNDRY

Guest Laundry—Schedule 8a

	Current Period
REVENUE	$
ALLOWANCES	————
NET REVENUE	
EXPENSES	
Salaries and Wages	
Employee Benefits	————
Total Payroll and Related Expenses	————
Other Expenses	
Contract Services	
Laundry Supplies	
Operating Supplies	
Telecommunications	
Training	
Uniforms	
Other	————
Total Other Expenses	————
TOTAL EXPENSES	————
DEPARTMENTAL INCOME (LOSS)	$ ————

Guest Laundry—Schedule 8b
(where only one laundry is operated)

	Current Period
REVENUE	$
ALLOWANCES	————
NET REVENUE	
COST OF LAUNDERING	————
DEPARTMENTAL INCOME (LOSS)	$ ════

Guest Laundry—Schedule 8 illustrates a format and identifies line items that commonly appear on a supplemental schedule supporting the Net Revenue, Payroll and Related Expenses, Other Expenses, and Income (Loss) amounts reported on the Summary Statement of Income for Operated Departments—Guest Laundry. This format and the line items will vary according to the needs and requirements of individual properties. Therefore, the line items listed on Schedule 8 may not apply to the operations of every property. Individual properties should modify Schedule 8 to meet their own needs and requirements.

Two formats are presented for the guest laundry operation. Where a distinct separation of costs for guest laundry and housework is possible, Schedule 8a should be used as the format to present departmental operating results. Where, as is generally the case, no division of the cost of house and guest work is practical, Schedule 8b should be used. In this situation, a "cost of laundering" may be estimated using a cost per pound with the same amount reducing the cost of operating the house laundry, as reflected in House Laundry, Schedule 28.

These formats and line items will vary according to the needs and requirements of individual properties. Therefore, the line items listed on Schedules 8a or 8b may not apply to the laundry operations of every property. Individual properties should modify Schedules 8a or 8b to meet their own needs and requirements.

Revenue

Laundry Revenue includes all revenue derived from laundry services provided to guests or other outside parties. In cases where a commission is received from outside laundries for work done for the property's guests, the commission amount should be included with Rentals and Other Income, Schedule 14.

Allowances

Allowances includes rebates, refunds, and overcharges of revenue not known at the time of sale but adjusted at a later date.

Net Revenue

Net Revenue is calculated by subtracting Allowances from Revenue. The Net Revenue amount on Schedule 8 is the same amount that appears on the Summary Statement of Income in the Net Revenues column for Operated Departments—Guest Laundry.

Cost of Laundering

The Cost of Laundering may be estimated using a cost per pound as described in the statement above. The estimated cost per pound should be sufficient to include the cost of boxes, cardboard, shirt bands, shirt fronts, buttons, pins, tags, and laundry bags.

Expenses

Salaries and Wages

Salaries and Wages includes regular pay, overtime pay, vacation pay, sick pay, holiday pay, incentive pay, severance pay, and bonuses for employees of the guest laundry department. This line item should also include any expense associated with leased labor, but not contract labor, which should be charged to Contract Services. If leased labor expense is significant, a separate line item called Leased Labor should be created and listed immediately after Salaries and Wages. For a classification of employees included in the guest laundry department, see Salaries and Wages, Schedule 29.

Employee Benefits

Employee Benefits includes payroll taxes, payroll-related insurance expense, pension, and other payroll-related expenses applicable to the guest laundry department. The cost of meals furnished to employees whose salaries and wages are charged to the guest laundry department is also included in this expense item. (See Payroll Taxes and Employee Benefits, Schedule 30.)

Total Payroll and Related Expenses

Total Payroll and Related Expenses is calculated by adding Salaries and Wages to Employee Benefits. The Total Payroll and Related Expenses amount is the same amount that appears on the Summary Statement of Income in the Payroll and Related Expenses column for Operated Departments—Guest Laundry.

Other Expenses

This expense grouping includes significant guest laundry expenses. Items appearing under Other Expenses vary from property to property. Examples of items that commonly appear as Other Expenses follow.

Contract Services. Contract Services includes any expense associated with an activity that is normally charged to the department, but is now outsourced. Examples include equipment maintenance and service contracts related to the guest laundry department.

Laundry Supplies. The cost of supplies used for laundering purposes is included in this line item.

Operating Supplies. Operating Supplies includes the cost of supplies used in the guest laundry, excluding the materials used for laundering purposes as designated under Laundry Supplies above. Items included in this line are the cost of boxes, cardboard, shirt bands, shirt fronts, buttons, pins, tags, and laundry bags.

Telecommunications. Any telecommunications expenditures that can be directly related to the guest laundry should be charged to this account.

Training. Training includes costs other than time associated with training employees. Examples include the costs of training materials, supplies, and instructor fees.

Uniforms. Uniforms includes the cost or rental of uniforms for employees of the guest laundry department. This item also includes the costs of cleaning or repairing uniforms of guest laundry employees.

Other. Expenses of the guest laundry that do not apply to line items discussed previously are included in this item.

Total Other Expenses

Total Other Expenses is calculated by adding all items listed under Other Expenses. The Total Other Expenses amount on Schedule 8 is the same amount that appears on the Summary Statement of Income in the Other Expenses column for Operated Departments—Guest Laundry.

Total Expenses

Total Expenses is calculated by adding Total Payroll and Related Expenses to Total Other Expenses.

Departmental Income (Loss)

The income (or loss) of the guest laundry department on Schedule 8a is calculated by subtracting Total Expenses from Net Revenue. The income (or loss) of the guest laundry department on Schedule 8b is calculated by subtracting the Cost of Laundering from Net Revenue. The Departmental Income (Loss) amount on Schedule 8 is the same amount that appears on the Summary Statement of Income in the Income (Loss) column for Operated Departments—Guest Laundry.

HEALTH CENTER

Health Center—Schedule 9

	Current Period
REVENUE	$
ALLOWANCES	———————
NET REVENUE	
COST OF MERCHANDISE SOLD	———————
GROSS PROFIT (LOSS)	
EXPENSES	
Salaries and Wages	
Employee Benefits	———————
Total Payroll and Related Expenses	———————
Other Expenses	
Contract Services	
Laundry and Dry Cleaning	
Licenses	
Linen	
Maintenance	
Operating Supplies	
Professional Services	
Telecommunications	
Training	
Uniforms	
Other	———————
Total Other Expenses	———————
TOTAL EXPENSES	———————
DEPARTMENTAL INCOME (LOSS)	$ ═══════

Health Center—Schedule 9 illustrates a format and identifies line items that commonly appear on a supplemental schedule supporting the Net Revenue, Cost of Sales, Payroll and Related Expenses, Other Expenses, and Income (Loss) amounts reported on the Summary Statement of Income for Operated Departments—Health Center. This format and the line items will vary according to the needs and requirements of individual properties. Therefore, the line items listed on Schedule 9 may not apply to the operations of every property. Individual properties should modify Schedule 9 to meet their own needs and requirements.

Revenue

Health center Revenue includes all the revenue derived from membership and visitor fees, fitness consultations and programs, massages and treatments, sales of merchandise (such as skin care products and clothing), and fees for other services provided by the club. Separate categories should be used to identify significant revenue items.

Allowances

Allowances includes rebates, refunds, and overcharges of revenue not known at the time of sale but adjusted at a later date.

Net Revenue

Net Revenue is calculated by subtracting Allowances from Revenue. The Net Revenue amount is the same amount that appears on the Summary Statement of Income in the Net Revenues column for Operated Departments—Health Center.

Cost of Merchandise Sold

Properties usually take a monthly merchandise inventory. The Cost of Merchandise Sold is calculated by adding health center merchandise purchases to the value of inventory at the beginning of the month and then subtracting the value of inventory at the end of the month. Total health center merchandise purchases is calculated by subtracting trade discounts (but *not* cash discounts) from the purchase price of the merchandise and then adding transportation and delivery charges. If separate categories were used to identify significant Revenue items, these same categories should be used to list the related Cost of Merchandise Sold. The Cost of Merchandise Sold is the same amount that appears on the Summary Statement of Income in the Cost of Sales column for Operated Departments—Health Center.

Gross Profit (Loss)

The Gross Profit (Loss) amount is calculated by subtracting Cost of Merchandise Sold from Net Revenue.

Expenses

Salaries and Wages

Salaries and Wages includes regular pay, overtime pay, vacation pay, sick pay, holiday pay, incentive pay, severance pay, and bonuses for employees of the health center. This line item should also include any expense associated with leased labor, but not contract labor, which should be charged to Contract Services. If leased labor expense is significant, a separate line item called Leased Labor should be created and listed immediately after Salaries and Wages. For a classification of employees included in the health center, see Salaries and Wages, Schedule 29.

Employee Benefits

Employee Benefits includes payroll taxes, payroll-related insurance expense, pension, and other payroll-related expenses applicable to the health center. The cost of meals furnished to employees whose salaries and wages are charged to the health center is also included in this expense item. (See Payroll Taxes and Employee Benefits, Schedule 30.)

Total Payroll and Related Expenses

Total Payroll and Related Expenses is calculated by adding Salaries and Wages to Employee Benefits. The Total Payroll and Related Expenses amount is the same amount that appears on the Summary Statement of Income in the Payroll and Related Expenses column for Operated Departments—Health Center.

Other Expenses

This expense grouping includes significant health center expenses. Items appearing under Other Expenses vary from property to property. Examples of items that commonly appear as Other Expenses follow.

Contract Services. Contract Services includes any expense associated with an activity that is normally charged to the department, but is now outsourced. Examples include the cost of equipment maintenance and service contracts related to the health center.

Laundry and Dry Cleaning. Laundry and Dry Cleaning includes the cost of contracting outside laundries for services applicable to the operation of the health center. These costs are determined from bills and invoices sent from outside laundries. For expenses applicable to the health center from the property's laundry facility, see House Laundry, Schedule 28.

Licenses. Licenses includes the costs of all licenses and permits that are necessary to operate a health center.

Linen. The cost or rental of linens such as towels and mats used in the health center should be charged to this account.

Maintenance. The cost of maintaining health center equipment such as the whirlpool, sauna, steam room, or exercise equipment should be charged to this account.

Operating Supplies. The cost of supplies used in the health center should be charged to this account.

Professional Services. The cost of contract professionals engaged to provide fitness consultations and massages and to assist management in health center operations should be charged to this account.

Telecommunications. Any telecommunications expenditures that can be directly related to the health center should be charged to this account.

Training. Training includes costs other than time associated with training employees. Examples include the costs of training materials, supplies, and instructor fees.

Uniforms. Uniforms includes the cost or rental of uniforms for employees of the health center. This item also includes the costs of cleaning or repairing uniforms of health center employees.

Other. Expenses of the health center that do not apply to line items discussed previously are included in this line item.

Total Other Expenses

Total Other Expenses is calculated by adding all items listed under Other Expenses. The Total Other Expenses amount on Schedule 9 is the same amount that appears on the Summary Statement of Income in the Other Expenses column for Operated Departments—Health Center.

Total Expenses

Total Expenses is calculated by adding Total Payroll and Related Expenses to Total Other Expenses.

Departmental Income (Loss)

The income (or loss) of the health center is calculated by subtracting Total Expenses from Gross Profit (Loss). The Departmental Income (Loss) amount on Schedule 9 is the same amount that appears on the Summary Statement of Income in the Income (Loss) column for Operated Departments—Health Center.

SWIMMING POOL

Swimming Pool—Schedule 10

	Current Period
REVENUE	$
ALLOWANCES	————
NET REVENUE	
EXPENSES	
Salaries and Wages	
Employee Benefits	————
Total Payroll and Related Expenses	————
Other Expenses	
Chemicals	
Contract Services	
Laundry and Dry Cleaning	
Linen	
Operating Supplies	
Professional Services	
Telecommunications	
Training	
Uniforms	
Other	————
Total Other Expenses	————
TOTAL EXPENSES	————
DEPARTMENTAL INCOME (LOSS)	$ ————

Swimming Pool—Schedule 10 illustrates a format and identifies line items which commonly appear on a supplemental schedule supporting the Net Revenue, Payroll and Related Expenses, Other Expenses, and Income (Loss) amounts reported on the Summary Statement of Income for Operated Departments—Swimming Pool. This format and the line items will vary according to the needs and requirements of individual properties. Therefore, the line items listed on Schedule 10 may not apply to the operations of the swimming pool department of every property. Individual properties should modify Schedule 10 to meet their own needs and requirements.

Revenue

Swimming pool Revenue includes all revenue derived from rentals of cabanas, lockers, mats, lounges and towels, from membership and visitor fees, and from fees charged to guests for instructions. Separate categories should be used to identify significant revenue items.

Allowances

Allowances includes rebates, refunds, and overcharges of revenue not known at the time of sale but adjusted at a later date.

Net Revenue

Net Revenue is calculated by subtracting Allowances from Revenue. The Net Revenue amount is the same amount that appears on the Summary Statement of Income in the Net Revenues column for Operated Departments—Swimming Pool.

Expenses

Salaries and Wages

Salaries and Wages includes regular pay, overtime pay, vacation pay, sick pay, holiday pay, incentive pay, severance pay, and bonuses for employees of the swimming pool department. This line item should also include any expense associated with leased labor, but not contract labor, which should be charged to Contract Services. If leased labor expense is significant, a separate line item called Leased Labor should be created and listed immediately after Salaries and Wages. For a classification of employees included in the swimming pool department, see Salaries and Wages, Schedule 29.

Employee Benefits

Employee Benefits includes payroll taxes, payroll-related insurance expense, pension, and other payroll-related expenses applicable to the swimming pool department. The cost of meals furnished to employees whose salaries and wages are charged to the swimming pool department is also included in this expense item. (See Payroll Taxes and Employee Benefits, Schedule 30.)

Total Payroll and Related Expenses

Total Payroll and Related Expenses is calculated by adding Salaries and Wages to Employee Benefits. The Total Payroll and Related Expenses amount is the same amount that appears on the Summary Statement of Income in the Payroll and Related Expenses column for Operated Departments—Swimming Pool.

Other Expenses

This expense grouping includes significant swimming pool expenses. Items appearing under Other Expenses vary from property to property. Examples of items that commonly appear as Other Expenses follow.

Chemicals. The cost of chlorine and other purifying chemicals should be charged to this account.

Contract Services. Contract Services includes any expense associated with an activity that is normally charged to the department, but is now outsourced. Examples include maintenance and service contracts for cleaning the pool and maintaining the pumping equipment and operations.

Laundry and Dry Cleaning. Laundry and Dry Cleaning includes the cost of contracting outside laundries for services applicable to the operation of the swimming pool. These costs are determined from bills and invoices sent from outside laundries. For services applicable to the swimming pool department from the property's laundry facility, see House Laundry, Schedule 28.

Linen. The cost or rental of linens such as towels and mats used in the swimming pool should be charged to this account.

Operating Supplies. The cost of supplies used in the swimming pool should be charged to this account.

Professional Services. The cost of contract professionals engaged to assist management in operating the swimming pool should be charged to this account.

Telecommunications. Any telecommunications expenditures that can be directly related to the swimming pool department should be charged to this account.

Training. Training includes costs other than time associated with training employees. Examples include the costs of training materials, supplies, and instructor fees.

Uniforms. Uniforms includes the cost or rental of uniforms for employees of the swimming pool department. This item also includes the cost of cleaning or repairing uniforms for the swimming pool department.

Other. Expenses of the swimming pool department that do not apply to line items discussed previously are included in this line item.

Total Other Expenses

Total Other Expenses is calculated by adding all items listed under Other Expenses. The Total Other Expenses amount is the same amount that appears on the Summary Statement of Income in the Other Expenses column for Operated Departments—Swimming Pool.

Total Expenses

Total Expenses is calculated by adding Total Payroll and Related Expenses to Total Other Expenses.

Departmental Income (Loss)

The income (or loss) of the swimming pool department is calculated by subtracting Total Other Expenses from Net Revenue. The Departmental Income (Loss) amount on Schedule 10 is the same amount that appears on the Summary Statement of Income in the Income (Loss) column for Operated Departments—Swimming Pool.

TENNIS

Tennis—Schedule 11

	Current Period
REVENUE	$
ALLOWANCES	_____
NET REVENUE	
EXPENSES	
Salaries and Wages	
Employee Benefits	_____
Total Payroll and Related Expenses	_____
Other Expenses	
Contract Services	
Court Maintenance	
Nets and Tapes	
Operating Supplies	
Professional Services	
Telecommunications	
Tournament Expense	
Training	
Other	_____
Total Other Expenses	_____
TOTAL EXPENSES	_____
DEPARTMENTAL INCOME (LOSS)	$ _____

Tennis—Schedule 11 illustrates a format and identifies line items that commonly appear on a supplemental schedule supporting the Net Revenue, Payroll and Related Expenses, Other Expenses, and Income (Loss) amounts reported on the Summary Statement of Income for Operated Departments—Tennis. This format and the line items will vary according to the needs and requirements of individual properties. Therefore, the line items listed on Schedule 11 may not apply to the operations of the tennis department of every property. Individual properties should modify Schedule 11 to meet their own needs and requirements.

Revenue

Tennis Revenue includes all revenue derived from court fees, membership fees, equipment rentals and repairs, and tournament fees. Separate categories should be used to identify significant revenue items.

Allowances

Allowances includes rebates, refunds, and overcharges of revenue not known at the time of sale but adjusted at a later date.

Net Revenue

Net Revenue is calculated by subtracting Allowances from Revenue. The Net Revenue amount is the same amount that appears on the Summary Statement of Income in the Net Revenues column for Operated Departments—Tennis.

Expenses

Salaries and Wages

Salaries and Wages includes regular pay, overtime pay, vacation pay, sick pay, holiday pay, incentive pay, severance pay, and bonuses for employees of the tennis department. This line item should also include any expense associated with leased labor, but not contract labor, which should be charged to Contract Services. If leased labor expense is significant, a separate line item called Leased Labor should be created and listed immediately after Salaries and Wages. For a classification of employees included in the tennis department, see Salaries and Wages, Schedule 29.

Employee Benefits

Employee Benefits includes payroll taxes, payroll-related insurance expense, pension, and other payroll-related expenses applicable to the tennis department. The cost of meals furnished to employees whose salaries and wages are charged to the tennis department is also included in this expense item. (See Payroll Taxes and Employee Benefits, Schedule 30.)

Total Payroll and Related Expenses

Total Payroll and Related Expenses is calculated by adding Salaries and Wages to Employee Benefits. The Total Payroll and Related Expenses amount is the same amount that appears on the Summary Statement of Income in the Payroll and Related Expenses column for Operated Departments—Tennis.

Other Expenses

This expense grouping includes significant tennis department expenses. Items appearing under Other Expenses vary from property to property. Examples of items that commonly appear as Other Expenses follow.

Contract Services. Contract Services includes any expense associated with an activity that is normally charged to the department, but is now outsourced. Examples include the cost of equipment maintenance and service contracts related to the tennis department.

Court Maintenance. The various expenses incurred in maintaining the courts in playable condition should be charged to this account.

Nets and Tapes. The cost of nets and tapes as well as repairs to these items should be charged to this account.

Operating Supplies. The cost of supplies used in operating the tennis department should be charged to this account.

Professional Services. The cost of contract professionals engaged to assist management in tennis operations, tournaments, and promotions should be charged to this account.

Telecommunications. Any telecommunications expenditures that can be directly related to the tennis department should be charged to this account.

Tournament Expense. All expenses incurred in administering tennis tournaments should be charged to this account.

Training. Training includes costs other than time associated with training employees. Examples include the costs of training materials, supplies, and instructor fees.

Other. Expenses of the tennis department that do not apply to line items discussed previously are included in this line item.

Total Other Expenses

Total Other Expenses is calculated by adding all items listed under Other Expenses. The Total Other Expenses amount on Schedule 11 is the same amount that appears on the Summary Statement of Income in the Other Expenses column for Operated Departments—Tennis.

Total Expenses

Total Expenses is calculated by adding Total Payroll and Related Expenses to Total Other Expenses.

Departmental Income (Loss)

The income (or loss) of the tennis department is calculated by subtracting Total Expenses from Net Revenue. The Departmental Income (Loss) amount on Schedule 11 is the same amount that appears on the Summary Statement of Income in the Income (Loss) column for Operated Departments—Tennis.

TENNIS PRO SHOP

Tennis Pro Shop—Schedule 12

	Current Period
REVENUE	$
ALLOWANCES	_____
NET REVENUE	
COST OF MERCHANDISE SOLD	_____
GROSS PROFIT (LOSS)	
OTHER INCOME	
GROSS PROFIT (LOSS) AND OTHER INCOME	
EXPENSES	
Salaries and Wages	
Employee Benefits	_____
Total Payroll and Related Expenses	_____
Other Expenses	
Contract Services	
Operating Supplies	
Telecommunications	
Training	
Other	_____
Total Other Expenses	_____
TOTAL EXPENSES	_____
DEPARTMENTAL INCOME (LOSS)	$ _____

Tennis Pro Shop—Schedule 12 illustrates a format and identifies line items that commonly appear on a supplemental schedule supporting the Net Revenue, Cost of Sales, Payroll and Related Expenses, Other Expenses, and Income (Loss) amounts reported on the Summary Statement of Income for Operated Departments—Tennis Pro Shop. This format and the line items will vary according to the needs and requirements of individual properties. Therefore, the line items listed on Schedule 12 may not apply to the operations of the tennis pro shop of every property. Individual properties should modify Schedule 12 to meet their own needs and requirements.

Revenue

Revenue for the tennis pro shop includes all revenue derived from sales of tennis apparel, tennis balls, tennis rackets, and accessories. Separate categories should be used to identify significant revenue items.

Allowances

Allowances includes rebates, refunds, and overcharges of revenue not known at the time of sale but adjusted at a later date.

Net Revenue

Net Revenue is calculated by subtracting Allowances from Revenue. The Net Revenue amount is added to the Other Income amount to arrive at the amount that appears on the Summary Statement of Income in the Net Revenues column for Operated Departments—Tennis Pro Shop.

Cost of Merchandise Sold

Properties usually take a monthly inventory of pro shop merchandise. The Cost of Merchandise Sold is calculated by adding total pro shop merchandise purchases to the value of inventory at the beginning of the month and then subtracting the value of inventory at the end of the month. Total pro shop merchandise purchases is calculated by subtracting trade discounts (but *not* cash discounts) from the purchase price of the merchandise and then adding transportation and delivery charges. If separate categories were used to identify significant Revenue items, these same categories should be used to list the related Cost of Merchandise Sold. The Cost of Merchandise Sold is the same amount that appears on the Summary Statement of Income in the Cost of Sales column for Operated Departments—Tennis Pro Shop.

Gross Profit (Loss)

The Gross Profit (Loss) amount is calculated by subtracting Cost of Merchandise Sold from Net Revenue.

Other Income

This account should be credited with revenue from other sources, such as stringing or repairing of guests' rackets. Other Income is added to Net revenue to arrive at the amount that appears in the Net Revenues column on the Summary Statement of Income for Operated Departments—Tennis Pro Shop.

Expenses

Salaries and Wages

Salaries and Wages includes regular pay, overtime pay, vacation pay, sick pay, holiday pay, incentive pay, severance pay, and bonuses for employees of the tennis pro shop. All commissions paid to the tennis pro or other employees of this department should be charged to this account. This line item should also include any expense associated with leased labor, but not contract labor, which should be charged to Contract Services. If leased labor expense is significant, a separate line item called Leased Labor should be created and listed immediately after Salaries and Wages. For a classification of employees included in the tennis pro shop, see Salaries and Wages, Schedule 29.

Employee Benefits

Employee Benefits includes payroll taxes, payroll-related insurance expense, pension, and other payroll-related expenses applicable to the tennis pro shop. The cost of meals furnished to employees whose salaries and wages are charged to the tennis pro shop is also included in this expense item. (See Payroll Taxes and Employee Benefits, Schedule 30.)

Total Payroll and Related Expenses

Total Payroll and Related Expenses is calculated by adding Salaries and Wages to Employee Benefits. The Total Payroll and Related Expenses amount is the same amount that appears on the Summary Statement of Income in the Payroll and Related Expenses column for Operated Departments—Tennis Pro Shop.

Other Expenses

This expense grouping includes significant tennis pro shop expenses. Items appearing under Other Expenses vary from property to property. Examples of items that commonly appear as Other Expenses follow.

Contract Services. Contract services includes any expense associated with an activity that is normally charged to the department, but is now outsourced. Examples include equipment maintenance and service contracts related to the tennis pro shop.

Operating Supplies. The cost of any supplies used in the tennis pro shop should be charged to this account.

Telecommunications. Any telecommunications expenditures that can be directly related to the tennis pro shop should be charged to this account.

Training. Training includes costs other than time associated with training employees. Examples include the costs of training materials, supplies, and instructor fees.

Other. Expenses of the tennis pro shop that do not apply to line items discussed previously are included in this line item.

Total Other Expenses

Total Other Expenses is calculated by adding all items listed under Other Expenses. The Total Other Expenses amount on Schedule 12 is the same amount that appears on the Summary Statement of Income in the Other Expenses column for Operated Departments—Tennis Pro Shop.

Total Expenses

Total Expenses is calculated by adding Total Payroll and Related Expenses to Total Other Expenses.

Departmental Income (Loss)

The income (or loss) for the tennis pro shop is calculated by subtracting Total Expenses from the sum of Gross Profit (Loss) and Other Income. The Departmental

Income (Loss) amount on Schedule 12 is the same amount that appears on the Summary Statement of Income in the Income (Loss) column for Operated Departments—Tennis Pro Shop.

OTHER OPERATED DEPARTMENTS

Other Operated Departments—Schedule 13

	Current Period
REVENUE	$
ALLOWANCES	————
NET REVENUE	
COST OF MERCHANDISE SOLD	————
GROSS PROFIT (LOSS)	
PAYROLL AND RELATED EXPENSES	
Salaries and Wages	
Employee Benefits	————
Total Payroll and Related Expenses	————
Other Expenses	
China and Glassware	
Contract Services	
Laundry	
Linen	
Operating Supplies	
Telecommunications	
Training	
Uniforms	
Other	————
Total Other Expenses	————
TOTAL EXPENSES	————
DEPARTMENTAL INCOME (LOSS)	$ ————

Many properties wish to offer their guests services and/or merchandise that are not provided by the operated departments discussed previously. In these cases, properties must decide whether the sale of such services and/or merchandise will be operated by departments within the facility or whether such operations will be contracted though rental or concession agreements. If a property decides to operate the sale of such services and/or merchandise, a separate schedule should be prepared for each of these areas of operations. Examples of other operated departments are as follows:

Barber/Beauty Shop
Children's Camp
Equestrian
Gift/Apparel Shop
Newsstand
Package Store
Show Room/Special Events
Sundry/Drug Store

Other Operated Departments—Schedule 13 illustrates a format and identifies line items that commonly appear on a supplemental schedule supporting the Net Revenue, Cost of Sales, Payroll and Related Expenses, Other Expenses, and Income (Loss) amounts reported on the Summary Statement of Income for Operated Departments. This format and the line items will vary according to the needs and requirements of individual properties. Therefore, the line items listed on this schedule may not apply to every other operated department that may exist within a property. Individual properties should modify this schedule to meet their own needs and requirements.

Revenue

Revenue for any other operated department is derived from the sale of services and/or merchandise applicable to that department. Properties may classify the items appearing under Revenue according to their individual needs and requirements. If, in relation to the total revenue generated by this department, a significant amount of revenue is generated by the sale of an item or by a group of similar items, the item or category should be listed separately under Revenue—Services or under Revenue—Sales of Merchandise.

Allowances

Allowances includes rebates, refunds, and overcharges of revenue not known at the time of sale but adjusted at a later date.

Net Revenue

Net Revenue is calculated by subtracting Allowances from Revenue. The Net Revenue amount on this schedule is the same amount that appears on the Summary Statement of Income in the Net Revenues column for Operated Departments.

Cost of Merchandise Sold

Properties usually take a monthly merchandise inventory. The Cost of Merchandise Sold for other operated departments is calculated by adding the total purchases amount to the value of inventory at the beginning of the period and then subtracting the value of inventory at the end of the period. The total purchases amount is calculated by subtracting trade discounts (but *not* cash discounts) from the purchase price of merchandise and then adding transportation and delivery charges. If individual items or categories of similar items are listed separately under Revenue—Sales of Merchandise, these same items or categories of items should also be listed separately under Cost of Merchandise Sold.

The Cost of Merchandise Sold amount on this schedule is the same amount that appears on the Summary Statement of Income in the Cost of Sales column for Operated Departments.

Gross Profit (Loss)

The Gross Profit (Loss) amount is calculated by subtracting Cost of Merchandise Sold from Net Revenue.

Expenses

Salaries and Wages

Salaries and Wages includes regular pay, overtime pay, vacation pay, sick pay, holiday pay, incentive pay, severance pay, and bonuses for employees of other operated departments. This line item should also include any expense associated with leased labor, but not contract labor, which should be charged to Contract Services. If leased labor expense is significant, a separate line item called Leased Labor should be created and listed immediately after Salaries and Wages.

Employee Benefits

Employee Benefits includes payroll taxes, payroll-related insurance expense, pension, and other payroll-related expenses applicable to other operated departments. The cost of meals furnished to employees whose salaries and wages are charged to other operated departments is also included in this expense item. (See Payroll Taxes and Employee Benefits, Schedule 30.)

Total Payroll and Related Expenses

Total Payroll and Related Expenses is calculated by adding Salaries and Wages to Employee Benefits. The Total Payroll and Related Expenses amount on this schedule is the same amount that appears on the Summary Statement of Income in the Payroll and Related Expenses column for Operated Departments.

Other Expenses

This expense grouping includes significant expenses of other operated departments. Items appearing under Other Expenses vary from property to property. Examples of items that may appear as Other Expenses include: china and glassware, contract services, laundry and dry cleaning, linen, operating supplies, telecommunications, training, uniforms, and other.

Total Other Expenses

Total Other Expenses is calculated by adding all items listed under Other Expenses. The Total Other Expenses amount is the same amount that appears on the Summary Statement of Income in the Other Expenses column for Operated Departments.

Total Expenses

Total Expenses is calculated by adding Total Payroll and Related Expenses to Total Other Expenses.

Departmental Income (Loss)

The income (or loss) of other operated departments is calculated by subtracting Total Expenses from Gross Profit (Loss). The Departmental Income (Loss) amount on this schedule is the same amount that appears on the Summary Statement of Income in the Income (Loss) column for Operated Departments.

RENTALS AND OTHER INCOME

Rentals and Other Income—Schedule 14	
	Current Period
Space Rentals and Concessions	$ _____
Commissions	
Cash Discounts Earned	
Cancellation Penalty	
Foreign Currency Transactions Gains (Losses)	
Interest Income	
Other	_____
TOTAL RENTALS AND OTHER INCOME	$ _____

Rentals and Other Income—Schedule 14 illustrates a format and identifies line items that commonly appear on a supplemental schedule supporting the Net Revenue and Income (Loss) amounts reported on the Summary Statement of Income for Operated Departments—Rentals and Other Income. This format and the line items will vary according to the needs and requirements of individual properties. Therefore, the line items listed on Schedule 14 may not apply to the rentals and other income operations of every property. Individual properties should modify Schedule 14 to meet their own needs and requirements.

Space Rentals and Concessions

Many properties wish to offer their guests services and/or merchandise that are not provided by the operated departments previously discussed. In these cases, properties contract the operations of such activities through rental or concession agreements. Space Rentals and Concessions includes the revenue generated from the rental of space within the property. The space rented may house activities traditionally operated by a property itself as part of its usual guest service offerings or may be for a business totally unrelated to the property. Separate categories should be used to identify significant revenue items.

Commissions to renting agents should be amortized over the term of the leases and charged against the gross income from rentals under each classification. The schedule may include only the net rentals, or preferably the gross rentals, commissions and expenses and the resulting net rentals.

Commissions

This line item should be credited with commissions received from others for services, such as communications, taxicab, garage and parking lot, automobile rentals, and photography. Separate categories should be used to identify significant revenue items. If a communications company occupies space in the property, the income to the property from such space should be credited to rentals even though the income is determined on the percentage basis. Similarly, so-called "commissions" from concessionaires should be included in the income from concessions. Income from unowned games and vending machines would also be included here.

Cash Discounts Earned

This account should be credited with the discount earned by the payment of creditors' accounts within the discount period, but should not be credited with trade discounts which are more properly a deduction from cost of merchandise sold.

Cancellation Penalty

This account should be credited with the income derived from forfeited deposits for property accommodations and services.

Foreign Currency Transactions Gains (Losses)

This account should include the foreign currency gains or losses from exchanging foreign currency into the local currency of the country that the property uses to report its results of operations.

Interest Income

This account should be credited with interest earned on cash investments, bank deposits, notes receivable, accounts receivable, and from other sources.

Other

This account should include items not classified under other captions.

Total Rentals and Other Income

The Total Rentals and Other Income is the same amount that appears on the Summary Statement of Income in both the Net Revenues and the Income (Loss) columns for Operated Departments—Rentals and Other Income.

ADMINISTRATIVE AND GENERAL

Administrative and General—Schedule 15

	Current Period
PAYROLL AND RELATED EXPENSES	
Salaries and Wages	$
Employee Benefits	_____
Total Payroll and Related Expenses	_____
OTHER EXPENSES	
Bank Charges	
Cash Overages and Shortages	
Communication Systems	
Contract Services	
Credit and Collection	
Credit Card Commissions	
Donations	
Dues and Subscriptions	
Head Office	
Human Resources	
Information Systems	
Internal Audit	
Internal Communications	
Loss and Damage	
Meals and Entertainment	
Operating Supplies and Equipment	
Postage	
Printing and Stationery	
Professional Fees	
Provision for Doubtful Accounts	
Security	
Telecommunications	
Training	
Transportation	
Travel	
Other	_____
Total Other Expenses	_____
TOTAL ADMINISTRATIVE AND GENERAL EXPENSES	$ _____

Administrative and General—Schedule15 illustrates a format and identifies line items that commonly appear on a supplemental schedule supporting the Payroll and Related Expenses and Other Expenses amounts reported on the Summary Statement of Income for Undistributed Operating Expenses—Administrative and General. These expenses are considered applicable to the entire property and are not easily allocated to operated departments. This format and the line items will vary according to the needs and requirements of individual properties. Therefore, the line items listed on Schedule 15 may not apply to the operations of every property. Individual properties should modify Schedule 15 to meet their own needs and requirements.

Expenses

Salaries and Wages

Salaries and Wages includes regular pay, overtime pay, vacation pay, sick pay, holiday pay, incentive pay, severance pay, and bonuses for employees of the administrative and general department. This line item should also include any expense associated with leased labor, but not contract labor, which should be charged to Contract Services. If leased labor expense is significant, a separate line item called Leased Labor should be created and listed immediately after Salaries and Wages. For a classification of employees included in the administrative and general department, see Salaries and Wages, Schedule 29.

Employee Benefits

Employee Benefits includes payroll taxes, payroll-related insurance expense, pension, and other payroll-related expenses applicable to the administrative and general department. The cost of meals furnished to employees whose salaries and wages are charged to the administrative and general department is also included in this expense item. (See Payroll Taxes and Employee Benefits, Schedule 30.)

Total Payroll and Related Expenses

Total Payroll and Related Expenses is calculated by adding Salaries and Wages to Employee Benefits. The Total Payroll and Related Expenses amount is the same amount that appears on the Summary Statement of Income in the Payroll and Related Expenses column for Undistributed Operating Expenses—Administrative and General.

Other Expenses

This expense grouping includes significant administrative and general department expenses. Items appearing under Other Expenses vary from property to property. Examples of items that commonly appear as Other Expenses follow.

Bank Charges. Bank charges assessed for miscellaneous banking services and transactions such as overdrafts, stop payments, check charges, and other related items should be charged to this account.

Cash Overages and Shortages. Cashiers' overages and shortages should be recorded in this account.

Communication Systems. Costs related to communication equipment such as telex and facsimile machines, radios, beepers, pagers, and cellular phones purchased for use by property employees, including related supplies and peripheral equipment, should be charged to this account.

Contract Services. Contract Services includes any expense associated with an activity that is normally charged to the department but is now outsourced. Examples include the cost of equipment maintenance contracts or other service contracts related specifically to the administrative and general department.

Credit and Collection. This account should be charged with the cost of collecting guest accounts, including attorney's fees and credit and check verification services.

Credit Card Commissions. This account is charged with the amount of commissions paid to credit card organizations. Volume rebate payments received from credit card organizations should also be credited to this account.

Donations. Charitable contributions should be charged to this account.

Dues and Subscriptions. The cost of representation of the property, or of members of the staff when authorized to represent the property, in business or professional organizations should be charged to this account. It also should be charged with the cost of subscriptions to newspapers, magazines, and books for use by the property staff.

Head Office. The portion of administrative salaries and expenses billed to the property by the head office should be charged to this account. The cost of meals and other applicable services or amenities provided to head office staff while on business in the property for the benefit of the property should also be charged to this account.

Human Resources. This account should include the cost of recruitment and relocation. If this item is significant, refer to Human Resources, Schedule 16.

Information Systems. The cost of management information system services, supplies, and equipment (excluding equipment rental and capital items) should be charged to this account. This includes minor equipment, software, supplies, peripheral equipment, and maintenance. To the extent practicable, these costs should be charged to the user department. If this item is significant, refer to Information Systems, Schedule 17.

Internal Audit. This account should include the cost of internal audits billed by the head office.

Loss and Damage. Payments made for guest property lost or damaged in excess of the amounts recovered from insurance companies should be charged to this account, as well as settlement of claims for damages.

Internal Communications. This account should be charged with the cost of duplication, pagers, dictation equipment, facsimile equipment, word processing, electronic mail, or other internal communications systems, including applicable supplies.

Meals and Entertainment. This item includes the reimbursable portion of any meal and entertainment expenses incurred by officers of the property.

Operating Supplies and Equipment. The cost of general office supplies such as photocopiers, adding machines, calculators, electric staplers, pencil sharpeners, and other similar equipment and related supplies, excluding equipment rental and capital items, should be charged to this account when used by, or purchased for, departments or employees whose salaries or wages are charged to the administrative and general department.

Postage. This account should be charged with the cost of postage, except amounts attributable to marketing.

Printing and Stationery. The cost of printed forms and stationery, whether purchased from outside printing concerns or produced internally, should be charged to this account when used by, or purchased for, departments or employees whose salaries or wages are charged to the administrative and general department.

Professional Fees. The cost of attorneys, public accountants, and professional consultants, including fees, travel, and other reimbursable expenses, should be charged to this account. Some properties may prefer to establish separate line items for significant professional fees categories (i.e., legal; external audit; consultants).

Provision for Doubtful Accounts. A charge adequate to provide for the probable loss in collection of accounts and notes receivable should be made to this account.

Security. This line item should include the cost of contract security and other related expenses. If significant, refer to Security, Schedule 18.

Telecommunications. Any telecommunications expenditures that can be directly related to the administrative and general department should be charged to this account.

Training. Training includes costs other than time associated with training employees. Examples include the costs of training materials, supplies, and instructor fees.

Transportation. This account should include the cost of transportation other than that directly related to guests. If there is a separate Human Resources department, this expense as it relates to employee transportation should be included in that department. If transportation expenses are significant, refer to Transportation, Schedule 20.

Travel. The cost of travel and reimbursable expenses of officers and employees of the property, traveling on the property's business, should be charged to this account, except that traveling in connection with business promotion should be charged to Marketing.

Other. Any administrative and general expenses that do not apply to line items discussed previously should be included in this line item.

Total Other Expenses

Total Other Expenses is calculated by adding all items listed under Other Expenses. The Total Other Expenses amount is the same amount that appears on the Summary Statement of Income in the Other Expenses column for Undistributed Operating Expenses—Administrative and General.

Total Administrative and General Expenses

Total Administrative and General Expenses is calculated by adding Total Payroll and Related Expenses and Total Other Expenses. Total Administrative and General Expenses on this schedule is the same amount that appears on the Summary Statement of Income in the Income (Loss) column for Undistributed Operating Expenses—Administrative and General.

HUMAN RESOURCES

Human Resources—Schedule 16

	Current Period
PAYROLL AND RELATED EXPENSES	
Salaries and Wages	$
Employee Benefits	_____
Total Payroll and Related Expenses	_____
OTHER EXPENSES	
Contract Services	
Dues and Subscriptions	
Employee Housing	
Employee Relations	
Medical Expenses	
Operating Supplies and Equipment	
Printing and Stationery	
Recruitment	
Relocation	
Telecommunications	
Training	
Transportation	
Other	_____
Total Other Expenses	_____
TOTAL HUMAN RESOURCES EXPENSES	$ _____

Human Resources—Schedule 16 illustrates a format and identifies line items that commonly appear on a supplemental schedule supporting the Payroll and Related Expenses and Other Expenses amounts reported on the Summary Statement of Income for Undistributed Operating Expenses—Human Resources.

For properties where commitments to human resources in terms of personnel and other expenses are significant, consideration should be given to establishing a separate department. For those properties that do not meet this requirement, human resources expenses should be included within administrative and general expenses. This format and the line items will vary according to the needs and requirements of individual properties. Therefore, the line items listed on Schedule 16 may not apply to the operations of every property. Individual properties should modify Schedule 16 to meet their own needs and requirements.

Expenses

Salaries and Wages

Salaries and Wages includes regular pay, overtime pay, vacation pay, sick pay, holiday pay, incentive pay, severance pay, and bonuses for employees of the human resources department. This line item should also include any expense associated with leased labor, but not contract labor, which should be charged to Contract Services. If leased labor expense is significant, a separate line item called Leased Labor should be created and listed immediately after Salaries and Wages.

For a classification of employees included in the human resources department, see Salaries and Wages, Schedule 29.

Employee Benefits

Employee Benefits includes payroll taxes, payroll-related insurance expense, pension, and other payroll-related expenses applicable to the human resources department. The cost of meals furnished to employees whose salaries and wages are charged to the human resources department is also included in this expense item. (See Payroll Taxes and Employee Benefits, Schedule 30.)

Total Payroll and Related Expenses

Total Payroll and Related Expenses is calculated by adding Salaries and Wages to Employee Benefits. The Total Payroll and Related Expenses amount is the same amount that appears on the Summary Statement of Income in the Payroll and Related Expenses column for Undistributed Operating Expenses—Human Resources.

Other Expenses

This expense grouping includes significant human resources department expenses. Items appearing under Other Expenses vary from property to property. Examples of items that commonly appear as Other Expenses follow.

Contract Services. Contract Services includes any expense associated with an activity that is normally charged to the department, but is now outsourced. Examples include temporary staff contracts and service contracts related to the human resources department.

Dues and Subscriptions. This account should be charged with the cost of memberships, subscriptions to newspapers and magazines, and books for use by employees in the human resources department.

Employee Housing. This account should be charged with the cost of providing housing, both temporary and permanent, for employees.

Employee Relations. Employee Relations includes all expenses associated with the cost of house media, social and sports activities, employee awards, and other such events and activities intended to improve employee relations and morale.

Medical Expenses. Physicians' fees and medical supplies should be charged to this account.

Operating Supplies and Equipment. The cost of general office supplies and minor equipment such as adding machines, calculators, electric staplers, pencil sharpeners, and other similar equipment and related supplies, excluding equipment rental and capital items, should be charged to this account when used by, or purchased for, the human resources department.

Printing and Stationery. The cost of printed forms, personnel manuals, and other printed materials, whether purchased from outside printing concerns or produced internally, should be charged to this account.

Recruitment. The cost of recruiting employees, including help wanted advertising, recruitment/placement fees, and expense reimbursement to candidates, should be charged to this account.

Relocation. This account should be charged with the cost of relocating employees. Examples of costs include transportation, moving and storage of household goods, temporary living expenses, real estate commissions, duplicate living expenses, mortgage differential payments, tax equalization payments, and similar items.

Telecommunications. Any telecommunications expenditures that can be directly related to the human resources department should be charged to this account.

Training. Training includes costs other than time associated with training employees. Examples include the costs of training materials, supplies, and instructor fees.

Transportation. Transportation should be charged with the cost of providing employee transportation.

Other. Expenses of the human resources department that do not apply to line items discussed previously are included in this line item.

Total Other Expenses

Total Other Expenses is calculated by adding all items listed under Other Expenses. The Total Other Expenses amount is the same amount that appears on the Summary Statement of Income in the Other Expenses column for Undistributed Operating Expenses—Human Resources.

Total Human Resources Expenses

Total Human Resources Expenses is calculated by adding Total Payroll and Related Expenses and Total Other Expenses. Total Human Resources Expenses on this schedule is the same amount that appears on the Summary Statement of Income in the Income (Loss) column for Undistributed Operating Expenses—Human Resources.

INFORMATION SYSTEMS

Information Systems—Schedule 17

	Current Period
PAYROLL AND RELATED EXPENSES	
Salaries and Wages	$ _____
Employee Benefits	_____
Total Payroll and Related Expenses	_____
OTHER EXPENSES	
Contract Services	
Equipment Maintenance	
Operating Supplies	
Printing and Stationery	
Software—Commercial Applications	
Telecommunications	
Training	
Other	_____
Total Other Expenses	_____
TOTAL INFORMATION SYSTEM EXPENSES	$ _____

Information Systems—Schedule 17 illustrates a format and identifies line items that commonly appear on a supplemental schedule supporting the Payroll and Related Expenses and Other Expenses amounts reported on the Summary Statement of Income for Undistributed Operating Expenses—Information Systems.

For properties with significant investments in data processing equipment under the responsibility of information system (IS) or management information system (MIS) professionals, consideration should be given to establishing a separate department. For those properties that do not meet this requirement, information system expenses will continue to be classified within the administrative and general department. This format and the line items will vary according to the needs and requirements of individual properties. Therefore, the line items listed on Schedule 17 may not apply to the operations of every property. Individual properties should modify Schedule 17 to meet their own needs and requirements.

Expenses

Salaries and Wages

Salaries and Wages includes regular pay, overtime pay, vacation pay, sick pay, holiday pay, incentive pay, severance pay, and bonuses for employees of the information systems department. This line item should also include any expense associated with leased labor, but not contract labor, which should be charged to Contract Services. If leased labor expense is significant, a separate line item called Leased Labor should be created and listed immediately after Salaries and Wages. For a classification of employees included in the information systems department, see Salaries and Wages—Schedule 29.

Employee Benefits

Employee Benefits includes payroll taxes, payroll-related insurance expense, pension, and other payroll-related expenses applicable to the information systems department. The cost of meals furnished to employees whose salaries and wages are charged to the information systems department is also included in this expense item. (See Payroll Taxes and Employee Benefits, Schedule 30.)

Total Payroll and Related Expenses

Total Payroll and Related Expenses is calculated by adding Salaries and Wages to Employee Benefits. The Total Payroll and Related Expenses amount is the same amount that appears on the Summary Statement of Income in the Payroll and Related Expenses column for Undistributed Operating Expenses—Information Systems.

Other Expenses

This expense grouping includes significant information systems department expenses. Items appearing under Other Expenses vary from property to property. Examples of items that commonly appear as Other Expenses follow.

Contract Services. Contract Services includes any expense associated with an activity that is normally charged to the department, but is now outsourced. Examples include computer equipment maintenance contracts and other service contracts related to the information systems department.

Equipment Maintenance. Equipment Maintenance should be charged with any direct maintenance to computer systems, including software and peripheral equipment. Some properties may prefer to charge these costs to a separate repairs and maintenance account in Property Operation and Maintenance, Schedule 21.

Operating Supplies. The cost of office supplies and computer and peripheral supplies such as diskettes, tape cartridges, printer toner cartridges, keyboards, surge suppressors, screen protectors, mice, tape drives, and other similar related supplies, excluding equipment rental and capital items, should be charged to this account when used by, or purchased for, information systems department employees. Similar items purchased for use by other departments or employees should be charged to their respective departments.

Printing and Stationery. The cost of printed forms, books, service manuals, stationery, and other printed materials, whether purchased from outside printing concerns or produced internally, should be charged to this account.

Software—Commercial Applications. The cost of "off-the-shelf" software applications purchased for use by information systems department employees should be charged to this account. "Off-the-shelf" software applications purchased for use by other departments or employees should be charged to their respective departments. Software upgrades that are not capitalized should also be charged to this account.

Telecommunications. Any telecommunications expenditures that can be directly related to the information systems department should be charged to this account.

Training. Training includes costs other than time associated with training employees. Examples include the costs of training materials, supplies, and instructor fees.

Other. Expenses of the information systems department that do not apply to line items discussed previously are included in this line item.

Total Other Expenses

Total Other Expenses is calculated by adding all items listed under Other Expenses. The Total Other Expenses amount is the same amount that appears on the Summary Statement of Income in the Other Expenses column for Undistributed Operating Expenses—Information Systems.

Total Information System Expenses

Total Information System Expenses is calculated by adding Total Payroll and Related Expenses and Total Other Expenses. Total Information System Expenses is the same amount that appears on the Summary Statement of Income in the Income (Loss) column for Undistributed Operating Expenses—Information Systems.

SECURITY

Security—Schedule 18

	Current Period
PAYROLL AND RELATED EXPENSES	
Salaries and Wages	$ _____
Employee Benefits	_____
Total Payroll and Related Expenses	_____
OTHER EXPENSES	
Armored Car Service	
Contract Services	
Operating Supplies	
Safety and Lock Boxes	
Telecommunications	
Training	
Uniforms	
Other	_____
Total Other Expenses	_____
TOTAL SECURITY EXPENSES	$ _____

Security—Schedule 18 illustrates a format and identifies line items that commonly appear on a supplemental schedule supporting the Payroll and Related Expenses and Other Expenses amounts reported on the Summary Statement of Income for Undistributed Operating Expenses—Security. This format and the line items will vary according to the needs and requirements of individual properties.

For properties where security expenses are significant, consideration should be given to establishing a separate department. For those properties that do not meet this requirement, security expenses should be included within administrative and general expenses. Individual properties should modify Schedule 18 to meet their own needs and requirements.

Expenses

Salaries and Wages

Salaries and Wages includes regular pay, overtime pay, vacation pay, sick pay, holiday pay, incentive pay, severance pay, and bonuses for employees of the security department. This line item should also include any expense associated with leased labor, but not contract labor, which should be charged to Contract Services. If leased labor expense is significant, a separate line item called Leased Labor should be created and listed immediately after Salaries and Wages. For a classification of employees included in the security department, see Salaries and Wages, Schedule 29.

Employee Benefits

Employee Benefits includes payroll taxes, payroll-related insurance expense, pension, and other payroll-related expenses applicable to the security department. The cost of meals furnished to employees whose salaries and wages are charged to the security department is also included in this expense item. (See Payroll Taxes and Employee Benefits, Schedule 30.)

Total Payroll and Related Expenses

Total Payroll and Related Expenses is calculated by adding Salaries and Wages to Employee Benefits. The Total Payroll and Related Expenses amount is the same amount that appears on the Summary Statement of Income in the Payroll and Related Expenses column for Undistributed Operating Expenses—Security.

Other Expenses

This expense grouping includes significant security department expenses. Items appearing under Other Expenses vary from property to property. Examples of items that commonly appear as Other Expenses follow.

Armored Car Service. The cost of transporting bank deposits and change from property to banking institution should be charged to this line item.

Contract Services. Contract Services includes any expense associated with an activity that is normally charged to the department, but is now outsourced. Examples include the cost of providing security service for the property, including special events and the costs of maintenance contracts on surveillance systems and guest locking systems.

Operating Supplies. The cost of badges, night sticks, handcuffs, flashlights, etc., should be charged to this line item.

Safety and Lock Boxes. The cost of maintenance on guest lock boxes and vaults should be charged to this line item.

Telecommunications. Any telecommunications expenditures that can be directly related to the security department should be charged to this line item.

Training. Training includes costs other than time associated with training employees. Examples include the costs of training materials, supplies, and instructor fees.

Uniforms. Uniforms includes the cost of specialized uniforms, including jackets, hats, and clothing for the security department. This item also includes the costs of cleaning or repairing uniforms of the security department.

Other. Expenses of the security department that do not apply to the line items discussed previously are included in this line item.

Total Other Expenses

Total Other Expenses is calculated by adding all items listed under Other Expenses. The Total Other Expenses amount is the same amount that appears on the

Summary Statement of Income in the Other Expenses column for Undistributed Operating Expenses—Security.

Total Security Expenses

Total Security Expenses is calculated by adding Total Payroll and Related Expenses and Total Other Expenses. Total Security Expenses is the same amount that appears on the Summary Statement of Income in the Income (Loss) column for Undistributed Operating Expenses—Security.

MARKETING AND FRANCHISE FEES

Marketing—Schedule 19

	Current Period
SELLING	
PAYROLL AND RELATED EXPENSES	
Salaries and Wages	$
Employee Benefits	_____
Total Payroll and Related Expenses	_____
OTHER EXPENSES	
Complimentary Guests	
Contract Services	
Dues and Subscriptions	
Meals and Entertainment	
Printing and Stationery	
Postage	
Trade Shows	
Telecommunications	
Training	
Travel	
Other	_____
Total Other Expenses	_____
TOTAL SELLING EXPENSES	
ADVERTISING AND MERCHANDISING	
PAYROLL AND RELATED EXPENSES	
Salaries and Wages	
Employee Benefits	_____
Total Payroll and Related Expenses	_____
OTHER EXPENSES	
Collateral Material	
Contract Services	
Direct Mail	
Frequent Stay Programs	
In-House Graphics	
Media	
Outdoor	
Point-of-Sale Material	
Special Promotional Vouchers	
Telecommunications	
Other	_____
Total Other Expenses	_____
TOTAL ADVERTISING AND MERCHANDISING EXPENSES	
FEES AND COMMISSIONS	
Agency Fees	
Other	_____
Total Fees and Commissions	
OTHER MARKETING EXPENSES	_____
TOTAL MARKETING EXPENSES	$ _____

Franchise Fees—Schedule 19a

	Current Period
FRANCHISE FEES	$ _____

Marketing—Schedule 19 illustrates a format and identifies line items that commonly appear on a supplemental schedule supporting the Payroll and Related Expenses and Other Expenses amounts reported on the Summary Statement of Income for Undistributed Operating Expenses—Marketing. This group of accounts should be charged with the costs incurred in connection with the creation and maintenance of the image of the property and the development, promotion, and furthering of new business. This format and the line items will vary according to the needs and requirements of individual properties. Therefore, the line items listed on Schedule 19 may not apply to the marketing operations of every property. Individual properties should modify Schedule 19 to meet their own needs and requirements.

Total Payroll and Related Expenses
(Selling and Advertising and Merchandising)

Salaries and Wages

Salaries and Wages includes regular pay, overtime pay, vacation pay, sick pay, holiday pay, incentive pay, severance pay, and bonuses for employees of the marketing department. This line item should also include any expense associated with leased labor, but not contract labor, which should be charged to Contract Services. If leased labor expense is significant, a separate line item called Leased Labor should be created and listed immediately after Salaries and Wages. For a classification of employees included in the marketing department, see Salaries and Wages, Schedule 29.

Employee Benefits

Employee Benefits includes payroll taxes, payroll-related insurance expense, pension, and other payroll-related expenses applicable to the marketing department. The cost of meals furnished to employees whose salaries and wages are charged to the marketing department is also included in this expense item. (See Payroll Taxes and Employee Benefits, Schedule 30.)

Total Payroll and Related Expenses

Total Payroll and Related Expenses is calculated by adding Salaries and Wages to Employee Benefits. The calculation for salaries and wages and employee benefits attributable to employees engaged in selling activities is performed separately from the calculation for those engaged in advertising and merchandising activities. Total Payroll and Related Expenses associated with selling activities is added to Total Payroll and Related Expenses associated with advertising and merchandising and the sum is the amount that appears on the Summary Statement of Income in the Payroll and Related Expenses column for Undistributed Operating Expenses—Marketing.

Other (Selling) Expenses

Complimentary Guests. This account is charged with the cost of providing guests with complimentary services that arise from selling and promotional activities.

Contract Services. Contract Services includes any expense associated with an activity that is normally charged to the department, but is now outsourced. Examples include equipment maintenance and other service contracts related to selling activities of the marketing department.

Dues and Subscriptions. This account includes the cost of memberships, subscriptions to newspapers and magazines, and books for use by employees in the marketing department.

Meals and Entertainment. This item includes the reimbursable portion of any meal and entertainment expenses incurred by marketing employees as part of their selling and promotional activities.

Printing and Stationery. The cost of sales manuals, printed forms, stationery, and office supplies, whether purchased from outside printing concerns or produced internally, should be charged to this account.

Postage. This account includes the cost of postage and shipping attributable to selling activities.

Trade Shows. This line item includes the cost of promoting the property at various trade shows, including travel and subsistence of attending representatives, cost of the booth, promotional logo items, and rental of exhibition space.

Telecommunications. Any telecommunications expense that can be directly related to selling activities should be charged to this account.

Training. Training includes costs other than time associated with training employees. Examples include the costs of training materials, supplies, and instructor fees.

Travel. This account includes the cost of transportation and reimbursable expenses of employees and officers engaged in sales promotion and the cost of entertaining for the purpose of promoting business.

Other. Expenses of the marketing department related to selling that do not apply to line items discussed previously are included in this line item.

Total Other Expenses

Total Other Expenses related to selling is calculated by adding all items listed under Other Expenses. Total Other Expenses associated with selling is added to Total Other Expenses associated with advertising and merchandising plus Total Fees and Commissions plus Total Other Marketing Expenses to arrive at the amount that appears on the Summary Statement of Income in the Other Expenses column for Undistributed Operating Expenses—Marketing.

Total Selling Expenses

Total Selling Expenses is calculated by adding Total Payroll and Related Expenses and Total Other Expenses.

Other (Advertising and Merchandising) Expenses

Collateral Material. This line item includes the cost of brochures, salespersons' kits, maps, floor plans, and similar materials used to describe the property's services.

Contract Services. Contract Services includes any expense associated with an activity that is normally charged to the department, but is now outsourced. Examples include equipment maintenance contracts and other service contracts related to advertising and merchandising activities of the marketing department.

Direct Mail. This line item includes the cost of mailing lists, letter writing, postage, addressing envelopes or cards, and other work of this nature completed by outside concerns.

Frequent Stay Programs. Any costs associated with programs designed to build guest loyalty to the property or brand should be charged to this account. Costs associated with cooperative frequent traveler programs, such as frequent flyer programs, could also be charged to this account.

In-House Graphics. This line item includes the cost of directories, signs, brochures, and other costs associated with merchandising the services of the property. Computer software programs and applications purchased to produce these items in-house should be charged to this account.

Media. The cost of advertising on radio and television, including production costs, as well as advertising in newspapers, magazines, and directories should be charged to this account.

Outdoor. The cost of posters, painted billboards, reader boards, and other signs, including rental costs and service charges, should be charged to this account.

Point-of-Sale Material. The cost of menu flyers and inserts, tent cards, and similar devices used to stimulate sales should be charged to this account.

Special Promotional Vouchers. This account includes any expenses, at the property's cost, associated with vouchers issued to guests for services rendered by the property.

Telecommunications. Any telecommunications expenditures that can be directly related to advertising and merchandising activities should be charged to this account.

Other. Expenses of the marketing department related to advertising and merchandising that do not apply to line items discussed previously are included in this line item.

Total Other Expenses

Total Other Expenses related to advertising and merchandising is calculated by adding all items listed under Other Expenses. Total Other Expenses related to advertising and merchandising is added to Total Other Expenses related to selling plus Total Fees and Commissions plus Total Other Marketing Expenses to arrive at the amount that appears on the Summary Statement of Income in the Other Expenses column for Undistributed Operating Expenses—Marketing.

Total Advertising and Merchandising Expenses

Total Advertising and Merchandising Expenses is calculated by adding Total Payroll and Related Expenses and Total Other Expenses.

Fees and Commissions

Agency Fees

This account is charged with fees paid to advertising and/or public relations agencies.

Other

Fees or commissions paid to persons who develop business for the property that are not included under agency fees should be charged to this account.

Total Fees and Commissions

Total Fees and Commissions is calculated by adding Agency Fees and Other. Total Fees and Commissions is added to Total Other Expenses associated with selling activities plus Total Other Expenses associated with advertising and merchandising activities plus Total Other Marketing Expenses to arrive at the amount that appears on the Summary Statement of Income in the Other Expenses column for Undistributed Operating Expenses—Marketing.

Other Marketing Expenses

This item includes all marketing expenses not discussed previously, including the following:

Civic and Community Activities. The cost of convention bureau activities, contribution to convention funds, or promotion of civic and community projects should be charged to this account.

Guest History. This account includes the cost of analyzing guest history data.

Outside Services. The cost of analysis prepared by independent research or consulting firms in order to determine demographic characteristics of the property's business are charged to this account.

Photography. This account includes the cost of photographs used in various types of promotional and publicity programs, including the cost of using professional models.

Other. Miscellaneous costs pertaining to the creation and maintenance of the public image of the property and incurred in market research activities that are not included under any other caption should be charged to this account.

Total Other Marketing Expenses

This total is calculated by adding all items listed above. The Total Other Marketing Expenses is added to Total Other Expenses for selling plus Total Other Expenses for advertising promotion plus Total Fees and Commissions to arrive at the amount that appears on the Summary Statement of Income in the Other Expenses column for Undistributed Operating Expenses—Marketing.

Total Marketing Expenses

Total Marketing Expenses is calculated by adding Total Selling Expenses plus Total Advertising and Merchandising Expenses plus Total Fees and Commissions plus Total Other Marketing Expenses. Total Marketing Expenses is the same amount that appears on the Summary Statement of Income in the Income (Loss) column for Undistributed Operating Expenses—Marketing.

Franchise Fees

Franchise Fees includes all fees charged by the franchise company, including royalties, fees for national advertising, and fees associated with the administration of frequent guest stay or similar programs.

TRANSPORTATION

Transportation—Schedule 20	
	Current Period
PAYROLL AND RELATED EXPENSES	
Salaries and Wages	$
Employee Benefits	_____
Total Payroll and Related Expenses	_____
OTHER EXPENSES	
Contract Services	
Fuel and Oil	
Insurance	
Operating Supplies	
Repairs and Maintenance	
Telecommunications	
Training	
Uniforms	
Other	_____
Total Other Expenses	_____
TOTAL TRANSPORTATION EXPENSES	$ _____

Transportation—Schedule 20 illustrates a format and identifies line items that commonly appear on a supplemental schedule supporting the Payroll and Related Expenses and Other Expenses amounts reported on the Summary Statement of Income for Undistributed Operating Expenses—Transportation. Properties that have significant expenses associated with guest transportation should consider establishing a separate transportation department. Those properties that do not meet this requirement should continue to classify transportation as a rooms department expense as suggested by Schedule 1. If the property generates significant revenue from transportation activities, it should create a separate schedule under operated departments. This format and the line items will vary according to the needs and requirements of individual properties. Therefore, the line items listed on Schedule 20 may not apply to the transportation operations of every property. Individual properties should modify Schedule 20 to meet their own needs and requirements.

Expenses

Salaries and Wages

Salaries and Wages includes regular pay, overtime pay, vacation pay, sick pay, holiday pay, incentive pay, severance pay, and bonuses for employees of the transportation department. This line item should also include any expense associated with leased labor, but not contract labor, which should be charged to Contract Services. If leased labor expense is significant, a separate line item called Leased Labor should be created and listed immediately after Salaries and Wages. For a classification of employees included in the transportation department, see Salaries and Wages, Schedule 29.

Employee Benefits

Employee Benefits includes payroll taxes, payroll-related insurance expense, pension, and other payroll-related expenses applicable to the transportation department. The cost of meals furnished to employees whose salaries and wages are charged to the transportation department is also included in this expense item. (See Payroll Taxes and Employee Benefits, Schedule 30.)

Total Payroll and Related Expenses

Total Payroll and Related Expenses is calculated by adding Salaries and Wages to Employee Benefits. The Total Payroll and Related Expenses amount is the same amount that appears on the Summary Statement of Income in the Payroll and Related Expenses column for Undistributed Operating Expenses—Transportation.

Other Expenses

This expense grouping includes significant transportation department expenses. Items appearing under Other Expenses vary from property to property. Examples of items that commonly appear as Other Expenses follow.

Contract Services. Contract Services includes any expense associated with an activity that is normally charged to the department, but is now outsourced. Examples include limousine services and fleet detailing services.

Fuel and Oil. This item includes the cost of fuel and oil directly used by vehicles owned or leased by the property.

Insurance. This item includes the cost of insurance on vehicles owned or leased by the property.

Operating Supplies. This item includes the cost of various supplies used in the transportation department.

Repairs and Maintenance. This item includes the cost of supplies, materials, and services associated with the repair and maintenance of vehicles owned or leased by the property.

Telecommunications. Any telecommunications expense that can be directly related to the transportation department should be charged to this account.

Training. Training includes costs other than time associated with training employees. Examples include the costs of training materials, supplies, and instructor fees.

Uniforms. Uniforms includes the cost or rental of uniforms for employees of the transportation department. This expense item also includes costs of cleaning or repairing uniforms of transportation department employees.

Other. Expenses of the transportation department that do not apply to line items discussed previously are included in this line item.

Total Other Expenses

Total Other Expenses is calculated by adding all items listed under Other Expenses. The Total Other Expenses amount is the same amount that appears on the Summary Statement of Income in the Other Expenses column for Undistributed Operating Expenses—Transportation.

Total Transportation Expenses

Total Transportation Expenses is calculated by adding Total Payroll and Related Expenses and Total Other Expenses. This amount is the same amount that appears on the Summary Statement of Income in the Income (Loss) column for Undistributed Operating Expenses—Transportation.

PROPERTY OPERATION AND MAINTENANCE

Property Operation and Maintenance—Schedule 21

	Current Period
PAYROLL AND RELATED EXPENSES	
Salaries and Wages	$
Employee Benefits	_____
Total Payroll and Related Expenses	_____
OTHER EXPENSES	
Building Supplies	
Contract Services	
Curtains and Draperies	
Electrical and Mechanical Equipment	
Elevators	
Engineering Supplies	
Floor Covering	
Furniture	
Grounds and Landscaping	
Heating, Ventilating, and Air Conditioning Equipment	
Kitchen Equipment	
Laundry Equipment	
Life/Safety	
Light Bulbs	
Locks and Keys	
Operating Supplies	
Painting and Decorating	
Removal of Waste Matter	
Swimming Pool	
Telecommunications	
Training	
Uniforms	
Vehicle Maintenance	
Other	_____
Total Other Expenses	_____
TOTAL PROPERTY OPERATION AND MAINTENANCE EXPENSES	$ _____

Property Operation and Maintenance—Schedule 21 illustrates a format and identifies line items that commonly appear on a supplemental schedule supporting the Payroll and Related Expenses and Other Expenses amounts reported on the Summary Statement of Income for Undistributed Operating Expenses—Property Operation and Maintenance. This format and the line items will vary according to the needs and requirements of individual properties. Therefore, the line items listed on Schedule 21 may not apply to the property operation and maintenance of every property. Individual properties should modify Schedule 21 to meet their own needs and requirements.

Expenses

Salaries and Wages

Salaries and Wages includes regular pay, overtime pay, vacation pay, sick pay, holiday pay, incentive pay, severance pay, and bonuses for employees of the property operation and maintenance department. This line item should also include any expense associated with leased labor, but not contract labor, which should be charged to Contract Services. If leased labor expense is significant, a separate line item called Leased Labor should be created and listed immediately after Salaries and Wages. For a classification of employees included in the property operation and maintenance department, see Salaries and Wages, Schedule 29.

Employee Benefits

Employee Benefits includes payroll taxes, payroll-related insurance expense, pension, and other payroll-related expenses applicable to the property operation and maintenance department. The cost of meals furnished to employees whose salaries and wages are charged to the property operation and maintenance department is also included in this expense item. (See Payroll Taxes and Employee Benefits, Schedule 30.)

Total Payroll and Related Expenses

Total Payroll and Related Expenses is calculated by adding Salaries and Wages to Employee Benefits. The Total Payroll and Related Expenses amount is the same amount that appears on the Summary Statement of Income in the Payroll and Related Expenses column for Undistributed Operating Expenses—Property Operation and Maintenance.

Other Expenses

This expense grouping includes significant property operation and maintenance department expenses. Items appearing under Other Expenses vary from property to property. Examples of items that commonly appear as Other Expenses follow.

Building Supplies. This line item includes any cost of material and contracts related to repairing and maintaining the building, both interior and exterior.

Contract Services. Contract Services includes any expense associated with an activity that is normally charged to the department, but is now outsourced. Examples include the equipment maintenance contracts and other service contracts related to this department.

Curtains and Draperies. This line item should be charged with the cost of materials and contracts related to repairing curtains and draperies.

Electrical and Mechanical Equipment. This line item should be charged with the cost of materials and contracts related to repairing and maintaining general equipment not specifically identified elsewhere. Maintenance contracts for specialized equipment such as telecommunications and data processing systems should be charged directly to the appropriate department.

Elevators. This line item should be charged with the cost of materials and contracts related to repairing and maintaining elevators.

Engineering Supplies. This line item should be charged with the maintenance and chemical supplies used in the property operation and maintenance department.

Floor Covering. This line item should be charged with the cost of materials and contracts related to repairing floor covering for guestrooms, corridors, dining rooms, and public rooms.

Furniture. This line item should be charged with the cost of contracts and materials and supplies such as textiles, fibers, lumber, metal parts, and glass related to the repair of furniture, including beds, tables, dressers, chairs, and other articles of similar nature.

Grounds and Landscaping. The cost of supplies and contracts related to the maintenance of grounds should be charged to this account.

Heating, Ventilating, and Air Conditioning Equipment. This line item should be charged with the cost of materials and contracts related to repairing and maintaining all heating, ventilating, and air conditioning equipment.

Kitchen Equipment. This line item should be charged with the cost of materials and contracts related to repairing and maintaining kitchen equipment.

Laundry Equipment. This line item should be charged with the cost of materials and contracts related to repairing and maintaining laundry equipment.

Life/Safety. This line item should be charged with the cost of regulatory inspection fees, certification tests, and materials and contracts to maintain fire control panels, tamper and flow switches, smoke detectors, and pull stations.

Light Bulbs. This line item should be charged with the cost of replacement light bulbs.

Locks and Keys. This line item should be charged with the cost of materials and contracts to maintain guestroom entry, panic hardware, safe deposit boxes, guestroom safes, etc.

Operating Supplies. The cost of various supplies used in the property operation and maintenance department should be charged to this line item.

Painting and Decorating. This line item should be charged with the cost of materials, supplies, and related contracts.

Removal of Waste Matter. The cost of the removal of rubbish and the expense of operating an incinerator should be charged to this line item.

Swimming Pool. This line item should be charged with the cost of materials, supplies, and contracts relating to the maintenance and repair of swimming pools when a separate department does not exist.

Telecommunications. Any telecommunications expenditures that can be directly related to the property operation and maintenance department should be charged to this account.

Training. Training includes costs other than time associated with training employees. Examples include the costs of training materials, supplies, and instructor fees.

Uniforms. Uniforms includes the cost or rental of uniforms for employees of the property operation and maintenance department. This expense item also includes costs of cleaning or repairing uniforms of property operation and maintenance department employees.

Vehicle Maintenance. This account includes the costs of maintaining property vehicles used for purposes other than guest transportation.

Other. Expenses of the property operation and maintenance department that do not apply to line items discussed previously are included in this line item.

Total Other Expenses

Total Other Expenses is calculated by adding all items listed under Other Expenses. The Total Other Expenses amount is the same amount that appears on the Summary Statement of Income in the Other Expenses column for Undistributed Operating Expenses—Property Operation and Maintenance.

Total Property Operation and Maintenance Expenses

Total Property Operation and Maintenance Expenses is calculated by adding Total Payroll and Related Expenses and Total Other Expenses. Total Property Operation and Maintenance Expenses is the same amount that appears on the Summary Statement of Income in the Income (Loss) column for Undistributed Operating Expenses—Property Operation and Maintenance.

UTILITY COSTS

Utility Costs—Schedule 22

	Current Period
UTILITY COSTS	
Electricity	$
Gas	
Oil	
Steam	
Water	
Other Fuels	
Total Utility Costs	————
RECOVERIES	
Recoveries from other entities	
Charges to other departments	————
Total Recoveries	————
NET UTILITY COSTS	$ ————

Utility Costs—Schedule 22 illustrates a format and identifies line items that commonly appear on a supplemental schedule supporting the Other Expenses amount reported on the Summary Statement of Income for Operated Departments—Utility Costs. This format and the line items will vary according to the needs and requirements of individual properties. Therefore, the line items listed on Schedule 22 may not apply to the operations of every property. If the property submeters utilities, the costs of these utilities may be charged to appropriate departments and reported on departmental schedules under Other Expenses. These costs are then included under Recoveries. Individual properties should modify Schedule 22 to meet their own needs and requirements.

Utility Costs

Electricity

The cost of electricity purchased from outside producers, including the cost of breakdown service, should be charged to this line item.

Gas

The cost of gas purchased from outside producers, including the cost of breakdown service, should be charged to this line item.

Oil

The cost of oil purchased from outside producers, including the cost of breakdown service, should be charged to this line item.

Steam

The cost of steam purchased from outside producers should be charged to this line item.

Water

This account should be charged with the cost of water consumed and should include water specially treated for the circulating ice water system, or purchased for drinking purposes. In addition, separate sewer charges should be included in this line item.

If the property has a cogeneration or desalinization plant, separate categories for these costs should be established.

Other Fuels

The cost of other fuels (for example, propane, diesel, geothermal) purchased from outside producers, including the cost of breakdown service, should be charged to this line item.

Total Utility Costs

Total Utility Costs is calculated by adding all of the items listed under Utility Costs.

Recoveries

Recoveries may be divided into two sections as follows:

Recoveries from Other Entities

This line item represents reimbursements from separate entities, such as managed condominiums, time-share units, or tenants of the property. If recoveries are from more than one source, they should be identified.

Charges to Other Departments

If a submetering capability for a comprehensive system for charging operated departments with utility costs is present, properties set up accounts in the respective departments and charge the costs to those departments. Allocation of utility costs when submetering does not exist should not be undertaken.

Total Recoveries

Total Recoveries is the sum of Recoveries from Other Entities and Charges to Other Departments.

Net Utility Costs

Net Utility Costs is calculated by subtracting Total Recoveries from Total Utility Costs. This sum is the same amount that appears on the Summary Statement of Income in both the Other Expenses and the Income (Loss) columns for Undistributed Operating Expenses—Utility Costs.

MANAGEMENT FEES

Management Fees—Schedule 23	
	Current Period
BASE FEES	$ _____
INCENTIVE FEES	_____
TOTAL MANAGEMENT FEES	$ _____

Management Fees—Schedule 23 details the fees charged by the organization managing the property for management services and supervision of the property.

Base Fees

Management fees computed as a fixed amount or a percentage of revenues or profit should be charged to this item.

Incentive Fees

Management fees that are contingent upon achieving certain pre-defined levels of profitability should be charged to this item.

Total Management Fees

Total Management Fees is the sum of Base Fees and Incentive Fees. This sum is the amount that appears on the Summary Statement of Income in the Income (Loss) column for Management Fees.

RENT, PROPERTY TAXES, AND INSURANCE

Rent, Property Taxes, and Insurance—Schedule 24

	Current Period
RENT	
Land and Buildings	$
Information Systems Equipment	
Telecommunications Equipment	
Other Property and Equipment	
Total Rent Expense	_____
PROPERTY TAXES	
Real Estate Taxes	
Personal Property Taxes	
Business and Transient Occupation Taxes	
Utility Taxes	
Other	
Total Property Tax Expense	_____
INSURANCE	
Building and Contents	
Liability	_____
Total Insurance	_____
TOTAL RENT, PROPERTY TAXES, AND INSURANCE	$ _____

Rent, Property Taxes, and Insurance—Schedule 24 details the expenses incurred by the property for rent, property taxes, and insurance.

Rent

Land and Buildings

If the property is leased under an operating lease, this line item should be charged with the amount of the rental of the property.

Information Systems Equipment

Rental of information systems and related hardware should be charged to this line item.

Telecommunications Equipment

This line item should be charged with the rental of telecommunications equipment.

Other Property and Equipment

Other rentals include rental of any other major items (for example, vehicles) which, had they not been rented, would be purchased and capitalized as property and equipment. Rental of miscellaneous equipment (copiers, projectors, and sound equipment) for a specific function, such as a banquet or similar function, should be charged to the appropriate department and is not to be considered rental expense chargeable to this line item.

Total Rent Expense

Total Rent Expense is calculated by adding all items listed under Rent.

Property Taxes

Real Estate Taxes

This account should be charged with all taxes assessed against the real property of the property by a state or political subdivision of the state, such as a county or city. Assessments for public improvements are not to be included in this line item as they are generally capitalized as property and equipment.

Personal Property Taxes

Taxes on furnishings, fixtures, and equipment should be charged to this line item.

Business and Transient Occupation Taxes

Taxes such as gross receipts tax on sale of rooms, food, and beverage that cannot be passed along to customers should be charged to this line item. In certain cases, the lodging facility may act as a conduit in the collection of taxes for the taxing authority.

Utility Taxes

Taxes assessed by utilities, such as sewer taxes, should be charged to this line item. Normal charges for refuse removal and utility services should be charged to Property Operation and Maintenance. Utility taxes related to the revenue generated from the resale of telecomunication services should be charged to the telecommunications department.

Other

Any taxes other than income and payroll taxes should be charged to this line item and separately identified if material.

Total Property Tax Expense

Total Property Tax Expense is calculated by adding all items listed under Property Taxes.

Insurance

Building and Contents

The cost of insuring the property's building and contents against damage or destruction by fire, weather, sprinkler leakage, boiler explosion, plate glass breakage, or any other cause should be charged to this account.

Liability

General insurance costs, including premiums relating to liability, fidelity, and theft coverage, should be charged to this account. These costs are typically controlled by the property owner and were charged to Administrative and General in previous editions of this book. Payroll-related insurance (workers' compensation) is included in Employee Benefits in the appropriate departmental schedule to which the associated payroll is charged.

Total Insurance

Total Insurance is calculated by adding all items listed under Insurance.

Total Rent, Property Taxes, and Insurance

Total Rent, Property Taxes, and Insurance is calculated by adding Total Rent Expense, Total Property Tax Expense, and Total Insurance. This sum is the amount that appears on the Summary Statement of Income in the Income (Loss) column for Rent, Property Taxes, and Insurance.

INTEREST EXPENSE

Interest Expense—Schedule 25

	Current Period
Amortization of Deferred Financing Costs	$
Mortgages	
Notes Payable	
Obligation Under Capital Leases	
Other Long-term Debt	
Other	_____
TOTAL INTEREST EXPENSE	$ =========

Interest Expense

Interest Expense—Schedule 25 includes all interest expenses incurred on any obligation such as mortgages, notes payable, bonds, debentures, taxes in arrears, or any other indebtedness on which interest is charged. The portion of lease payments under capital leases that represents interest on the outstanding balances of the obligations is also included in this schedule. Amortization of Deferred Financing Costs and other costs related to obtaining financing should be charged to this account over the estimated period of the related financing. Interest charges should be grouped into categories that indicate the nature of the principal indebtedness on which interest is incurred.

Total Interest Expense is the sum of all items listed on the schedule. The sum is the amount that appears on the Summary Statement of Income in the Income (Loss) column for Interest Expense.

DEPRECIATION AND AMORTIZATION

Depreciation and Amortization—Schedule 26	
	Current Period
Assets Held Under Capital Leases	$
Buildings	
Furnishings and Equipment	
Leaseholds and Leasehold Improvements	
Intangibles	
Other	_____
TOTAL DEPRECIATION AND AMORTIZATION	$ _____

Depreciation and Amortization—Schedule 26 details the categories in which the property has taken depreciation or amortization.

Depreciation and Amortization

Assets Held Under Capital Leases

Amortization of assets held under capital leases should be charged to this line item.

Buildings

Depreciation on the property's buildings and improvements should be charged to this line item over their estimated useful lives.

Furnishings and Equipment

Depreciation of furnishings and equipment should be charged to this line item over their estimated useful lives. The line item should include depreciation of china, glassware, silver, linen, and uniforms, when such items are not accounted for by the inventory method.

Leaseholds and Leasehold Improvements

The amortization of costs of acquiring leaseholds and leasehold improvements should be charged to this line item over the shorter of their estimated useful lives or their lease terms.

Intangibles

The amortization of intangibles, such as goodwill, should be charged to this line item over the period during which the intangible is expected to benefit the property.

Other

Depreciation and amortization of long-term assets that are not included in the above categories should be charged to this line item.

Total Depreciation and Amortization

Total Depreciation and Amortization is the sum of all items listed on the schedule. This sum is the amount that appears on the Summary Statement of Income in the Income (Loss) column for Depreciation and Amortization.

INCOME TAXES

Federal and State Income Taxes—Schedule 27

	Current Period
FEDERAL	
Current	
Deferred	$ _____
Total Federal	_____
STATE	
Current	_____
Deferred	_____
Total State	
TOTAL FEDERAL AND STATE INCOME TAXES	$ _____

All taxes that are assessed on the basis of the income earned by the property should be charged to these accounts. When there are differences between income reported for financial statement purposes and income reported for income tax purposes, the amount of income tax currently payable and the amount that has been deferred should be shown separately. Items that give rise to deferred income taxes include, but are not limited to, the difference in tax and book depreciation and items capitalized as property and equipment on the books but treated as an expense for tax purposes.

The Total Federal and State Income Taxes is the amount that appears on the Summary Statement of Income in the Income (Loss) column for Income Taxes.

HOUSE LAUNDRY

House Laundry—Schedule 28

		Current Period
PAYROLL AND RELATED EXPENSES		
Salaries and Wages		$ _____
Employee Benefits		_____
Total Payroll and Related Expenses		_____
OTHER EXPENSES		
Cleaning Supplies		
Contract Services		
Laundry Supplies		
Printing and Stationery		
Telecommunications		
Training		
Uniforms		
Other		_____
Total Other Expenses		_____
TOTAL EXPENSES		
CREDITS		
Cost of Guest and Outside Laundry		
Concessionaires' Laundry		
Total Credits		_____
COST OF HOUSE LAUNDRY		_____
CHARGED TO:		
Rooms	Schedule 1	
Food	Schedule 2	
Beverage	Schedule 3	
Golf Course	Schedule 6	
Health Center	Schedule 9	
Swimming Pool	Schedule 10	
Other Operated Departments	Schedule 13	_____
Total		$ _____

House Laundry—Schedule 28 illustrates a format and identifies line items that commonly appear on a supplemental schedule supporting the Payroll and Related Expenses and Other Expenses amounts reported for House Laundry that are allocated to various departments. This format and the line items will vary according to the needs and requirements of individual properties. Therefore, the line items listed on Schedule 28 may not apply to the house laundry operations of every property. Individual properties should modify Schedule 28 to meet their own needs and requirements.

Expenses

Salaries and Wages

Salaries and Wages includes regular pay, overtime pay, vacation pay, sick pay, holiday pay, incentive pay, severance pay, and bonuses for employees of the house laundry department. This line item should also include any expense associated with leased labor, but not contract labor, which should be charged to Contract Services. If leased labor expense is significant, a separate line item called Leased Labor should be created and listed immediately after Salaries and Wages. For a classification of employees included in the house laundry department, see Salaries and Wages, Schedule 29.

Employee Benefits

Employee Benefits includes payroll taxes, payroll-related insurance expense, pension, and other payroll-related expenses applicable to the house laundry. The cost of meals furnished to employees whose salaries and wages are charged to the house laundry department is also included in this expense item. (See Payroll Taxes and Employee Benefits, Schedule 30.)

Total Payroll and Related Expenses

Total Payroll and Related Expenses is calculated by adding Salaries and Wages to Employee Benefits.

Other Expenses

This expense grouping includes significant house laundry department expenses. Items appearing under Other Expenses vary from property to property. Examples of items that commonly appear as Other Expenses follow.

Cleaning Supplies. This line item is charged with the cost of supplies to keep the house laundry in a clean and sanitary condition. This account should not include materials described below used for laundering purposes.

Contract Services. Contract Services includes any expense associated with an activity that is normally charged to the department, but is now outsourced. Examples include equipment maintenance contracts and other service contracts related to the house laundry department.

Laundry Supplies. This line item is charged with the cost of supplies used for laundering purposes.

Printing and Stationery. The cost of laundry lists, printed forms, service manuals, stationery, and office supplies, whether purchased or produced internally, should be charged to this line item.

Telecommunications. Any telecommunications expenditures that can be directly related to the house laundry department should be charged to this line item.

Training. Training includes costs other than time associated with training employees. Examples include the costs of training materials, supplies, and instructor fees.

Uniforms. Uniforms includes the cost or rental of uniforms for employees of the house laundry department. This expense item also includes the costs of cleaning or repairing uniforms of house laundry department employees.

Other. Expenses of the house laundry department that do not apply to line items discussed previously are included in this line item.

Total Other Expenses

Total Other Expenses is calculated by adding all of the items listed under Other Expenses.

Total Expenses

Total Expenses for the house laundry is calculated by adding Total Payroll and Related Expenses and Total Other Expenses.

Credits

Cost of Guest and Outside Laundry

Where no separate guest laundry is maintained, this account should be credited with the number of pounds processed times the cost per pound, based on the total cost of production. (See Guest Laundry, Schedule 8.)

Concessionaires' Laundry

Where laundering is done for concessionaires such as barber/beauty shops, the revenue received is usually deducted from the departmental expenses.

Cost of House Laundry

The Cost of House Laundry is calculated by subtracting Total Credits from Total Expenses. The Cost of House Laundry should be distributed to Rooms, Food, Beverage, Golf Course, Health Center, Swimming Pool, and Other Operated Departments on a cost-per-pound basis.

SALARIES AND WAGES

Salaries and Wages—Schedule 29

	Number of Employees or Full-Time Equivalents	Current Period
ROOMS		
Management		$
Front Office		
House Attendants		
Housekeeper and Assistants		
Linen Control		
Reservations		
Service		
Total Rooms (Schedule 1)		
FOOD		
Management		
Food Preparation		
Food Service		
Restaurants		
Banquets		
Room Service		
Food General		
Total Food (Schedule 2)		
BEVERAGE		
Management		
Beverage Service		
Lounges		
Banquets		
Mini-Bars		
Total Beverage (Schedule 3)		
TELECOMMUNICATIONS (Schedule 4)		
GARAGE AND PARKING (Schedule 5)		
GOLF COURSE (Schedule 6)		
GOLF PRO SHOP (Schedule 7)		
GUEST LAUNDRY (Schedule 8)		
HEALTH CENTER (Schedule 9)		
SWIMMING POOL (Schedule 10)		
TENNIS (Schedule 11)		
TENNIS PRO SHOP (Schedule 12)		
OTHER OPERATED DEPARTMENTS (Schedule 13)		
ADMINISTRATIVE AND GENERAL		
Manager's Office		
Finance		
Accounting Department		
Guest Accounting		
Credit Department		
Revenue Night Auditors		
Food and Beverage Control		
Storeroom and Receiving		

Salaries and Wages—Schedule 29 *(continued)*

	Number of Employees or Full-Time Equivalents	Current Period
ADMINISTRATIVE AND GENERAL *(continued)*		
Purchasing		$
Total Administrative and General (Schedule 15)		
HUMAN RESOURCES (Schedule 16)		
INFORMATION SYSTEMS (Schedule 17)		
SECURITY (Schedule 18)		
MARKETING (Schedule 19)		
TRANSPORTATION (Schedule 20)		
PROPERTY OPERATION AND MAINTENANCE		
Carpenters and Furniture Repairers		
Carpet Repairers		
Chief Engineer and Assistants		
Electricians		
General Mechanical		
Grounds and Landscaping		
Kitchen Mechanics		
Masons		
Office, Storeroom and Other		
Painters and Paperhangers		
Plumbers and Steam Fitters		
Plant Operators		
Radio and Television		
Refrigeration		
Upholstery and Drapery Repairers		
Total Property Operation and Maintenance (Schedule 21)		
HOUSE LAUNDRY		
Finishing		
Manager and Assistants		
Washing		
Other		
Total House Laundry (Schedule 28)		
TOTAL SALARIES AND WAGES		$ _____

Salaries and Wages

Salaries and Wages—Schedule 29 illustrates a format and identifies line items that commonly appear on a supplemental schedule supporting the salaries and wages allocated to various departments. This format and the line items will vary according to the needs and requirements of individual properties. Therefore, the line items listed on Schedule 29 may not apply to the operations of every property. Individual properties should modify Schedule 29 to meet their own needs and requirements.

Rooms

Management

Rooms director, front office manager, assistant front office managers, secretary, director of guest services, guest service managers.

Front Office

Concierge, guest service agents.

House Attendants

Floor supervisors, room attendants, janitors, house attendants.

Housekeeper and Assistants

Housekeeper, assistant housekeeper, housekeeping secretary, clerks.

Linen Control

Linen control supervisor, linen room staff, sewing staff.

Reservations

Reservations manager, reservations supervisor, reservations agents.

Service

Concierge supervisor, concierge staff, bell captain, bellpersons, door attendants, elevator operators, lobby porters, bell phones.

Food

Management

Food director, director of catering, director of restaurants, assistant food/catering directors, secretaries to management.

Food Preparation

Executive chef, executive sous chef, pastry chef, assistant chefs, chef garde manger, chef tournant, butcher, baker supervisor, bakers, sauciers, pantry supervisor, pantry helpers, vegetable preparation staff, dish up, chief steward, stewarding supervisors, dishwashers, potwashers, silver room supervisor, silver room staff.

Food Service

Restaurants. Restaurant manager, assistant restaurant manager, maître d', supervisors, host/hostess, bus persons, server, food runners.

Banquets. Banquet manager, assistant banquet manager, banquet captain, banquet bus person, banquet server.

Room Service

Room service manager, assistant room service manager, room service order takers, servers, bus persons, room service captain.

Food General

Food cashier supervisor, food cashiers, catering sales manager, catering assistant, convention manager, assistant convention manager.

Beverage

Management

Beverage director, lounge manager, assistant beverage director.

Beverage Service

Lounge assistant manager, banquet bar manager, assistant banquet bar manager, public bartender, banquet bartender, barback, banquet barback, lounge server.

Mini-Bars

Manager, beverage runner, beverage stockers.

Telecommunications

Telecommunications manager, telecommunications supervisor, telephone operators, technicians.

Garage and Parking

Manager, supervisors, valet runners, drivers, mechanics, helpers, washers, cleaners, kiosk cashiers.

Golf Course

Maintenance

Greenskeeper and assistant, gardeners, general maintenance, drivers, mechanics.

Operations

Professional, assistant professional, caddy master, locker room attendant, club storage and repair attendant, golf car storage attendants, rangers, starters, caddies.

Golf Pro Shop

Manager, assistant, sales clerks.

Guest Laundry

Superintendent and assistant, clerks, bundle and hand washers, starchers, plain/fancy collar and shirt ironers, markers and sorters, delivery clerks.

Health Center

Manager, masseur/masseuse, attendant, steam room and sauna attendant.

Swimming Pool

Manager, cashiers and clerks, masseur/masseuse, attendants, porters, lifeguards, cabana attendants, steam room attendants, linen handlers.

Tennis

Professional, assistant, locker room attendants, sales clerks, maintenance workers.

Tennis Pro Shop

Manager, assistant, sales clerks.

Administrative and General

Manager's Office

Managing director, general manager, resident manager, executive assistant manager, night operations manager, secretaries, clerks, receptionists.

Finance

Chief financial officer, internal auditor, financial analyst, treasurer, budget analyst, secretary, clerks.

Accounting Department

Controller, assistant controller, accounting manager, general cashier, paymaster, payroll staff, staff accountants, income auditors, accounts payable supervisor and staff, clerks.

Guest Accounting

Accounts receivable supervisor, group billing staff, billing clerks, front office cashier supervisor, front office cashiers, file clerks.

Credit Department

Credit manager collection clerks, secretaries.

Revenue Night Auditors

Chief night auditor and staff, food and beverage night auditors.

Food and Beverage Control

Food and beverage cost controller and staff.

Storeroom and Receiving

Storeroom attendants, receiving clerks.

Purchasing

Director of purchasing, buyers, clerks.

Human Resources

Personnel director, employee relations representative, training director, counselors, secretaries, clerks.

Information Systems

Director of information systems, MIS manager, systems analysts, programmers, operators, data entry staff, if information processing is a separate department.

Security

Director of security, security officers, guards.

Marketing

Sales

Director of marketing, sales manager, convention service manager, sales representatives, secretaries, clerks.

Advertising and Merchandising

Advertising manager, artists, composers, secretaries, clerks.

Other Marketing Activities

Public relations manager, publicity manager, staff publicist, research analyst, guest history clerks, secretaries.

Transportation

Manager, drivers, mechanics, secretaries, clerks.

Property Operation and Maintenance

Carpenters and Furniture Repairers

Includes cabinet workers and wood finishers.

Carpet Repairers

Carpet layers and binders.

Chief Engineer and Assistants

Chief engineer and first assistant.

Electricians

Electricians, motor repairers, electrical distribution maintenance workers, lighting personnel.

General Mechanical

Elevator mechanics, machinists, locksmiths.

Grounds and Landscaping

Gardeners, laborers.

Kitchen Mechanics

Appliance repairers.

Masons

Includes setters and plasterers.

Office, Storeroom and Other

Storeroom clerks, secretaries and clerks in the engineer's office, cleaners, yard attendants, incinerator attendants.

Painters and Paperhangers

Includes sign painters.

Plumbers and Steam Fitters

Plumbers and assistants.

Plant Operators

Watch engineers, boiler room engineers, elevator engineers, air-conditioning control, energy management personnel.

Radio and Television

Repairers.

Refrigeration

Refrigeration mechanics, ice handlers.

Upholstery and Drapery Repairers

Upholstery and drapery repairers.

House Laundry

Finishing

Mangle workers, folders, curtain handlers, starchers, press machine operators, ironers, finishers, flat workers, shakers, feeders, receivers.

Manager and Assistants

Manager, assistant manager, clerks.

Washing

Washers, wringers, extractors, pullers, tumblers.

Other

Sorters, markers, checkers, collection and delivery employees, cleaners, utility workers, linen attendants, chute attendants, bundle workers, porters.

Casino

Casino manager, slot operations manager, table games manager, shift supervisors, pit bosses, floorpersons, boxpersons, dealers, stickpersons, security guards, cage cashiers, count team members.

PAYROLL TAXES AND EMPLOYEE BENEFITS

Payroll Taxes and Employee Benefits—Schedule 30

	Current Period
PAYROLL TAXES	
Federal Retirement (FICA)	$
Federal Unemployment (FUTA)	
Medicare (FICA)	
State Disability	
State Unemployment (SUTA)	————
Total Payroll Taxes	
EMPLOYEE BENEFITS	
Auto Allowance	
Child Care	
Contributory Savings Plan (401K)	
Dental Insurance	
Disability Pay	
Group Life Insurance	
Health Insurance	
Meals	
Nonunion Insurance	
Nonunion Pension	
Profit Sharing	
Stock Benefits	
Union Insurance	
Union Pension	
Workers' Compensation Insurance	
Other	————
Total Employee Benefits	————
TOTAL PAYROLL TAXES AND EMPLOYEE BENEFITS	$ ═══
Charged to	
Rooms	
Food	
Beverage	
Telecommunications	
Garage and Parking	
Golf Course	
Golf Pro Shop	
Guest Laundry	
Health Center	
Swimming Pool	
Tennis	
Tennis Pro Shop	
Other Operated Departments	
Administrative and General	
Human Resources	
Information Systems	
Security	
Marketing	
Transportation	
Property Operation and Maintenance	
House Laundry	
Total	$

Payroll Taxes and Employee Benefits—Schedule 30 illustrates a format and identifies line items that commonly appear on a supplemental schedule supporting the payroll taxes and employee benefits allocated to various departments. This format and the line items will vary according to the needs and requirements of individual properties. Therefore, the line items listed on Schedule 30 may not apply to the operations of every property. Individual properties should modify Schedule 30 to meet their own needs and requirements.

Payroll Taxes

Federal Retirement (FICA)

This account is to be charged with taxes imposed on employers by Subchapter B, Chapter 21, of the Internal Revenue Code.

Federal Unemployment (FUTA)

This account is to be charged with taxes imposed by Chapter 23 of the Internal Revenue Code.

Medicare (FICA)

This account is to be charged with taxes imposed on employers by Subchapter B, Chapter 21, of the Internal Revenue Code.

State Disability

This account is to be charged with contributions by employers to state agencies for disabilities purposes.

State Unemployment (SUTA)

This account is to be charged with contributions by employers to unemployment funds required by state unemployment compensation laws.

Employee Benefits

Auto Allowance

Cost of providing payment to employees for company-owned vehicles and flat allowances for use of autos.

Child Care

Cost of providing contracted care or in-house facilities for employees' children.

Contributory Savings Plan (401K)

Cost of employer's portion of programs with matching amounts and administrative costs.

Dental Insurance

Employer cost of dental insurance for employees less amounts reimbursed.

Disability Pay

Cost of providing disability pay to employees.

Group Life Insurance

Cost of group life insurance on employees.

Health Insurance

Employer cost of health insurance for employees.

Meals

Employer cost of providing meals to employees.

Nonunion Insurance

Cost of life, health, accident, hospitalization, and other insurance for employees not participating in a union fund.

Nonunion Pension

Costs associated with nonunion pension plans.

Profit Sharing

The cost of the employer's contribution to profit sharing plans.

Stock Benefits

Cost of providing employees with company stock.

Union Insurance

Costs associated with union employees' benefit funds for insurance on life, health, accident, hospitalization, and other purposes.

Union Pension

Costs associated with union employees' pension benefit funds.

Workers' Compensation Insurance

Cost of insurance for employee state compensation plans.

Other

Cost of providing employees with other benefits not included under other captions (i.e., daytimers {organizers}, name tags, seminars, organization dues, employee award and incentive parties, etc.).

Section 7
Statement for Gaming Operations

Casino Department

	Current Period
REVENUE	$
LESS COMPLIMENTARY ALLOWANCES	_____
NET REVENUE	
PAYROLL AND RELATED EXPENSES	
Salaries and Wages	
Employee Benefits	_____
Total Payroll and Related Expenses	_____
OTHER EXPENSES	
Complimentaries:	
Rooms	
Food	
Beverage	
Travel	
Special Events	
Other Amenities	
Contract Services	
Credit and Collection	
Gaming Taxes, License Fees, and Regulatory Costs	
Operating Supplies	
Postage	
Provision for Doubtful Accounts	
Telecommunications	
Training	
Uniforms	
Other	_____
Total Other Expenses	_____
TOTAL EXPENSES	_____
DEPARTMENTAL INCOME (LOSS)	$ _____

The Casino Department schedule is included for use by properties in which the casino is considered another form of recreation and entertainment offered by the property. As such, the casino department should be listed as another operated department on the Summary Statement of Income.

The casino department schedule shown here illustrates a format and identifies line items that commonly appear on a supplemental schedule supporting the Net Revenue, Payroll and Related Expenses, Other Expenses, and Income (Loss) amounts reported on the Summary Statement of Income for Operated Departments—Casino. This format and the line items will vary according to the needs and requirements of individual properties. Therefore, the line items listed on this schedule may not apply to the casino department of every property. Individual properties should modify the schedule to meet their own needs and requirements.

Revenue

These accounts should be credited with the revenue derived from table games, slot machines, and other gaming revenues. Table games generally include Blackjack or Twenty-one, Craps, Baccarat, Roulette, and Wheel of Fortune or Big Six. Other casino revenues may include Keno, Poker, and Race and Sports Book. Casino department revenue is defined as the difference between gaming wins and losses, not the total amount wagered.

Slot Machine Jackpots

Base jackpots represent the minimum amount to be paid for a specific combination of symbols appearing on the reels or other payoff mechanisms. Base jackpots may be deducted from gaming revenue when they are initially established if they are relatively insignificant to total gaming revenues. Alternatively, they may be deducted from revenue evenly over the period anticipated to occur prior to jackpot payout.

Jackpots for progressive slot machines increase as they are played, as indicated by a series of meters prominently displayed on the machine. The jackpot increases by a fixed amount as coins are played. The increase in the unpaid progressive liability is generally accrued currently by the casino with an offsetting reduction to gaming revenues for the period.

Participating Slot Machines

Some casinos do not own some or all of their slot machines and, instead, enter into participation agreements, which are similar to lease arrangements. The owner-lessor of the machines shares in a percentage of the profits from the slot operations after deducting any expenses specified in the participation agreement. The total participating slot machine win is generally recorded as casino revenue, while the participation payment is reflected as an expense of the casino department.

Complimentary Allowances

It is a prevalent gaming industry practice to provide gaming patrons Complimentary (also termed "Promotional") Allowances, including rooms, food, beverage, travel, and other amenities free of charge as an incentive to gamble at the property's casino. These goods and services are generally provided by hotel operating departments other than the casino. The approximate retail value of Complimentary Allowances is generally included in Revenue of the operating department providing the complimentary goods or services with a corresponding amount deducted as Complimentary Allowances from Casino Revenue to determine Net Revenue for gaming operations. Alternatively, the retail value of Complimentary Allowances may be excluded from Revenue, generally with disclosure in the notes to the financial statements of the approximate retail value of the Complimentary Allowances provided by each operating department.

Net Revenue

Net Revenue for the casino department is calculated by subtracting Complimentary Allowances from Revenue. The Net Revenue amount is the same amount that appears on the Summary Statement of Income in the Net Revenues column for Operated Departments—Casino.

Expenses

Salaries and Wages

Salaries and Wages includes regular pay, overtime pay, vacation pay, sick pay, holiday pay, incentive pay, severance pay, and bonuses for employees of the casino department. This line item should also include any expense associated with leased labor, but not contract labor, which should be charged to Contract Services. If leased labor expense is significant, a separate line item called Leased Labor should be created and listed immediately after Salaries and Wages. For a classification of employees included in this group, see Salaries and Wages, Schedule 29.

Employee Benefits

Employee Benefits includes payroll taxes, payroll-related insurance expense, pension, and other payroll-related expenses applicable to the casino department. The cost of meals furnished to employees whose salaries and wages are charged to the casino department is also included in this expense item. (See Payroll Taxes and Employee Benefits, Schedule 30.)

Total Payroll and Related Expenses

Total Payroll and Related Expenses is calculated by adding Salaries and Wages to Employee Benefits. The Total Payroll and Related Expenses amount is the same amount that appears on the Summary Statement of Income in the Payroll and Related Expenses column for Operated Departments—Casino.

Other Expenses

This expense grouping includes significant casino department expenses. Items appearing under Other Expenses vary from property to property. Examples of items that commonly appear as Other Expenses follow.

Complimentaries. This item includes the cost of providing rooms, food, beverage, travel, special events, and other amenities to guests at no charge. These expenses are reported either as an expense of the department providing the complimentary item or reclassified as a casino department expense. (The latter method is required by the Securities and Exchange Commission for public reporting companies in the United States.)

Contract Services. Contract Services includes any expense associated with an activity that is normally charged to the department, but is now outsourced. Examples include equipment maintenance contracts and other service contracts related to the casino department.

Credit and Collection. This item includes the cost of collecting casino accounts, related attorneys' fees, and credit background reports.

Gaming Taxes, License Fees, and Regulatory Costs. This item includes the cost of all federal, state, and municipal gaming licenses as well as taxes on casino revenues and gaming regulatory costs.

Operating Supplies. Operating supplies includes the cost of supplies used in the casino department such as chip racks, chip cups, coin wrappers, dice, dice cups, keno brushes, keno crayons, marker chips, playing cards, and roulette balls.

Postage. Any postage expenditures that can be directly related to the casino department should be charged to this account.

Provision for Doubtful Accounts. Some casinos may extend credit through the issuance of "markers" to gaming patrons, particularly those engaged in relatively high wagering limits. The Provision for Doubtful Accounts is a charge adequate to provide for the probable loss in collection of markers and other forms of gaming credit issued.

Telecommunications. Any telecommunications expenditures that can be directly related to the casino department should be charged to this account.

Training. Training includes costs other than time associated with training employees. Examples include the costs of training materials, supplies, and instructor fees.

Uniforms. Uniforms includes the cost or rental of uniforms for employees of the casino department. This item also includes the cost of cleaning or repairing uniforms for casino department employees.

Other. Expenses of the casino department that do not apply to line items discussed previously are included in this line item.

Total Other Expenses

Total Other Expenses is calculated by adding all items listed under Other Expenses. The Total Other Expenses amount on this schedule is the same amount that appears on the Summary Statement of Income in the Other Expenses column for Operated Departments—Casino.

Total Expenses

Total Expenses is calculated by adding Total Payroll and Related Expenses and Total Other Expenses.

Departmental Income (Loss)

The income (or loss) of the casino department is calculated by subtracting Total Expenses from Net Revenue. The Departmental Income (Loss) amount on this schedule is the same amount that appears on the Summary Statement of Income in the Income (Loss) column for Operated Departments—Casino.

Section 8
Statement for Properties
Operated by a Management Company

Many properties are operated under the terms of management contracts. In these instances, it is common for the owner of the lodging property to retain accounting control and responsibility for certain asset, liability, and operating accounts (generally property, debt, and related expenses), while requiring the management company to maintain the accounting for the other asset and liability accounts, generally those related to operations. The following guidelines are presented for the preparation of the Statement of Assets and Liabilities by the operator.

It is important to recognize that a Statement of Assets and Liabilities by the operator is a partial presentation and is not a representation of the balance sheet of a legal entity. The items included or excluded will be determined by the management agreement or by concurrence between the owner and the operator. It is recommended that the notes to the Statement of Assets and Liabilities clearly explain the limited nature of the statement presentation.

No attempt has been made to identify all the variations that might be found in the presentation of statements of assets and liabilities prepared by operators. Instead, more usual variations are discussed to give some guidance. Other items will be handled in a similar manner:

- If the owner retains accounting responsibility for property and equipment, no amounts for such items will be reflected in the Statement of Assets and Liabilities by the operator. If acquisitions are made from cash flow from operations and the owner maintains the accounting for property and equipment, the operator will charge the acquisition to the owner through the owner's control account.

- If the owner retains accounting responsibility for debt, the operator's Statement of Assets and Liabilities will likewise not reflect any debt. If the operator is responsible for debt service, the operator will charge the amount paid to the owner's control account.

- If the owner has the responsibility for funding working capital (in cash or in kind, such as inventory) or making other contributions, the operator will credit the amount received to the owner's control account. Distributions to the owner would similarly be charged to the owner's control account.

- It is common that management contracts require the establishment of a property and equipment replacement reserve. Typically, this reserve is based on a percentage of the hotel's revenue and may require the segregation of cash and the establishment of a separate cash escrow account. If the management agreement requires a reserve or escrow account for property and equipment replacements, the net unexpended restricted cash should be reflected as a noncurrent asset in the Statement of Assets and Liabilities. To the extent that the reserve is funded by the owner rather than through current operations, appropriate accounting would be made by use of the owner's control account.

- Operating income and losses will be credited or charged to the owner's control account. It is recommended that cumulative operating income and losses be shown as a separate item within the owner's control section of the Statement of Assets and Liabilities.

An illustration of a Statement of Assets and Liabilities for a property operated by a management company is presented on the next page. This Statement of Assets and Liabilities, when combined with the owner's Statement of Assets and Liabilities, will represent a complete balance sheet.

The description of the composition of the asset and liability accounts may be found in Section 1.

If a significant number of transactions are processed through the owner's control account, it is suggested that the notes to the Statement of Assets and Liabilities include a summarization of the individual items to allow easy reconciliation between the owner and the operator.

While the above discussion focuses on the Statement of Assets and Liabilities for a property operated by a management company, it is probable that the management company will prepare a full set of financial statements. Accordingly, one would expect to find a Statement of Assets and Liabilities and Statements of Revenue and Expenses and Cash Flow. These separate statements are not discussed in detail in this section because their format will be substantially similar to the statements discussed in detail previously.

The footnotes to the statements will contain the information applicable to statements prepared by properties as previously discussed. It is suggested that the details of the calculation of the management fee be presented in a footnote if it is significant to the statements.

Illustration of a
STATEMENT OF ASSETS AND LIABILITIES
for a Property Operated by a Management Company

Statement of Assets and Liabilities

	Current Year	Prior Year
Assets		
CURRENT ASSETS		
Cash		
House Banks	$	$
Demand Deposits		
Temporary Cash Investments		
Total Cash	$	$
Short-Term Investments		
Receivables		
Accounts Receivable		
Notes Receivable		
Other		
Total Receivables	$	$
Less Allowance for Doubtful Accounts		
Net Receivables	$	$
Inventories		
Prepaid Expenses		
Other		
Total Current Assets	$	$
PROPERTY AND EQUIPMENT		
PROPERTY AND EQUIPMENT ESCROW		
OTHER ASSETS		
Deferred Charges		
Other		
Total Other Assets	$	$
TOTAL ASSETS	$	$
Liabilities and Owner's Control		
CURRENT LIABILITIES	$	$
Notes Payable		
Accounts Payable		
Accrued Expenses		
Accrued Management Fees		
Advance Deposits		
Other		
Total Current Liabilities	$	$
DEFERRED MANAGEMENT FEES	$	$
OWNER'S CONTROL		
Net Contributions		
Owner's Income (Loss)		
Total Owner's Control	$	$
TOTAL LIABILITIES AND OWNER'S CONTROLER'S INCOME (LOSS)	$	$

Part II
Financial Analysis

Section 9
Financial Statement Formats

The formats of the Summary Statement of Income and departmental statements can of course be designed to provide only one amount column to record figures for the time period covered by the statement. While the primary purpose of any of these statements is to present the revenue and expenses for the most recent accounting period, the true significance of such amounts can only be fully understood when compared with budgets and/or the corresponding amounts for preceding periods. Accordingly, individual properties should modify the format of these statements to meet their needs and requirements. For example, properties may find it useful to expand this basic format by adding columns to provide:

- A comparative analysis of the current period results with the amounts budgeted for the period

- A comparative analysis of the current period results with those of the same period for the preceding year

- Cumulative year-to-date information

- Percentage relationships between revenue and expenses

Comparisons can be made by either horizontal or vertical analyses. Horizontal analysis indicates the absolute (dollar) and relative (percentage) differences between the two amounts of the same line items. The absolute differences are simply the dollar differences between the figures (this year and last year or actual and budget). The relative differences are percentage differences, and are calculated by dividing the absolute differences by the prior year or budget amounts. Vertical analysis uses net revenue as a common denominator and reduces the amount of each line on the respective income statements to a percentage. This analysis produces common-size statements that permit reasonable comparisons of two or more periods with different levels of activity.

The introduction of the microcomputer and the development of spreadsheet programs have greatly facilitated the generation of more complex income statement formats. The user need only enter current and prior period or budget information, and the computer can perform the necessary computations and format the statements.

Alternative Income Statement Format A presents a format that includes columns for both current period and year-to-date information and comparative figures. The comparative figures may be budget numbers or the results of the same period for the preceding year. A comparison to budget or forecast is preferred since this enables management to concentrate on the underlying business reasons that actual results exceeded or fell short of planned results. Comparisons with previous periods, although not as meaningful as comparisons with budgets, are useful for indicating the relative performance of current operations.

For those properties desiring a more complete presentation, *Alternative Income Statement Format B* includes a provision for both current period and year-to-date information as well as for comparison with both the budget and a prior period. In addition, a column has been provided to show the year-to-date dollar variance between actual results and the budget. In this instance, an explanatory analysis of the variance should accompany the financial statements.

When calculating the percentage columns of these alternative income statements, net revenue is normally used as the base and expenses are expressed as a percentage of net revenue. Properties may choose to show the percentages for all line items or only those for the more important items. In addition to reporting the percentage relationship between revenue and expenses, departmental schedules may also present statistical information regarding the efficiency of operations. Typical statistics associated with each of the departmental schedules is discussed in Section 11.

Alternative Income Statement Format A

Line Item Description	Current Month				Year-To-Date			
	Actual		Comparative		Actual		Comparative	
	Dollars	Percent	Dollars	Percent	Dollars	Percent	Dollars	Percent

Alternative Income Statement Format B

Current Month						Acct. No.	Line Item Description	Year-To-Date							
Actual		Budget		Prior Year				Actual		Budget			Prior Year		
Dollars	Percent	Dollars	Percent	Dollars	Percent			Dollars	Percent	Dollars	Percent	Variance	Dollars	Percent	

Section 10
Ratio Analysis and Statistics

The use of ratios and statistics as a basis of comparison, measurement, and communication is prevalent within the lodging industry. The usefulness of these tools is predicated on a commonality of definition and understanding. The various ratios and statistics that can be developed and be useful are numerous. The intent of this section is to provide a consistent, uniform definition of basic lodging industry ratios and statistics. This section includes only those ratios and statistics that are in widespread general use within the industry. It is not intended to be a complete listing and definition of all possible relevant ratios and statistics.

RATIO ANALYSIS

Financial statements issued by lodging properties contain a considerable amount of information. A thorough analysis of this information requires more than simply reading the reported figures and facts. Users of financial statements need to be able to interpret the figures and facts, and make them yield information that reveals aspects of the property's financial situation or operation that could otherwise go unnoticed. This is accomplished through ratio analysis, which compares related facts reported on financial statements. A ratio gives mathematical expression to a relationship between two figures, and is calculated by dividing one figure by the other.

Although ratios are critical to any financial analysis, they are only indicators and, as indicators, they are meaningful only when compared to useful criteria. Useful criteria with which to compare the results of ratio analysis include:

- The corresponding ratio calculated for a prior period
- Other properties and industry averages
- Planned ratio goals

Users of ratio analysis must be careful when comparing two different properties, because the accounting procedures used by the properties may differ and their ratios may not be comparable. Ratio analysis can be extremely useful to owners, creditors, and managers in evaluating the financial condition and operation of a lodging property. However, ratios are only indicators; they do not resolve problems or actually reveal what the problems may be. At best, when ratios vary significantly from past periods, budgeted standards, or industry averages, they indicate that problems may exist. When problems appear to exist, considerably more analysis and investigation is necessary to determine the appropriate corrective actions.

Liquidity Ratios

Liquidity ratios measure an operation's ability to meet its current, short-term obligations. Owners and stockholders often prefer relatively low current ratios because investments in many current assets may be less productive than investments in noncurrent assets. Creditors, on the other hand, normally prefer relatively high current ratios because this gives them assurance that the lodging property will be able to meet its short-term obligations. Management is caught in the middle, trying to satisfy both owners and creditors while maintaining adequate working capital and sufficient liquidity to ensure the smooth operation of the property.

Current Ratio

The most common liquidity ratio is the current ratio, which is the ratio of total current assets to total current liabilities. The current ratio can be calculated as follows:

$$\text{Current Ratio} = \frac{\text{Current Assets}}{\text{Current Liabilities}}$$

This ratio reveals the amount of current assets for every dollar of current liabilities.

Acid-Test Ratio

The acid-test ratio measures a property's liquidity by considering only "quick assets"—current assets minus inventories and prepaid expenses. This is often a more stringent measure of a property's liquidity because it may take several months for many properties to convert their inventories to cash. The acid-test ratio can be calculated as follows:

$$\text{Acid-Test Ratio} = \frac{\text{Quick Assets}}{\text{Current Liabilities}}$$

This ratio reveals the amount of quick assets for every dollar of current liabilities.

Accounts Receivable Turnover

Accounts receivable can be the largest current asset of lodging properties because credit is often extended to guests. Therefore, any examination of a property's liquidity must consider how quickly accounts receivable are converted to cash. This is determined by the accounts receivable turnover ratio, which divides total revenue by the average accounts receivable. A refinement of this ratio uses only charge sales in the numerator; however, quite often charge sales figures are unavailable. Regardless of whether total revenue or charge sales are used as the numerator, the calculation should be consistent from period to period.

To calculate the accounts receivable turnover, it is first necessary to determine the average accounts receivable. This is accomplished by adding accounts receivable at the beginning and end of the period and then dividing that figure by two. The average accounts receivable figure is then divided into the total revenue for the period. The accounts receivable turnover can be calculated as follows:

$$\text{Accounts Receivable Turnover} = \frac{\text{Total Revenue}}{\text{Average Accounts Receivable}}$$

Average Collection Period

This ratio reveals the number of days required to collect the average accounts receivable. The average collection period is calculated by dividing the number of days in the year by the accounts receivable turnover. The average collection period can be calculated as follows:

$$\text{Average Collection Period} = \frac{\text{Days in Year}}{\text{Accounts Receivable Turnover}}$$

Solvency Ratios

Solvency ratios measure the degree of debt financing used by the lodging property. These ratios reflect the ability of the property to meet its long-term obligations. Owners view solvency ratios as a measure of their leverage, and often prefer relatively low solvency ratios because their leverage increases as debt is used in place of equity dollars to increase the return on equity dollars already invested. Creditors, on the other hand, prefer relatively high solvency ratios because they reveal an equity cushion available to absorb any operating losses. Management is again caught in the middle, trying to satisfy owners by financing assets so as to maximize return on investments and trying to satisfy creditors by not unduly jeopardizing the property's ability to meet its long-term obligations.

Solvency Ratio

A lodging operation is solvent when its assets are greater than its liabilities. The solvency ratio compares total assets to total liabilities. The solvency ratio can be calculated as follows:

$$\text{Solvency Ratio} = \frac{\text{Total Assets}}{\text{Total Liabilities}}$$

This ratio reveals the amount of assets for every dollar of liabilities.

Debt-Equity Ratio

One of the most common solvency ratios is the debt-equity ratio, which compares the total debt of the operation to the total investment in the operation by the owners. The debt-equity ratio can be calculated as follows:

$$\text{Debt-Equity Ratio} = \frac{\text{Total Liabilities}}{\text{Total Owners' Equity}}$$

This ratio reveals the amount owed to creditors for every dollar of owners' equity.

Number of Times Interest Earned

This ratio expresses the number of times interest expense can be covered. The greater the number of times interest is earned, the greater the safety afforded creditors. The number of times interest earned ratio can be calculated as follows:

$$\text{Number of Times Interest Earned Ratio} = \frac{\text{Income Before Income Taxes} + \text{Interest Expense}}{\text{Interest Expense}}$$

Properties that obtain the use of property and equipment through leases may find the fixed charge coverage ratio to be more useful than the number of times interest earned ratio.

Fixed Charge Coverage Ratio

This ratio is a variation of the number of times interest earned ratio and is useful for those properties that have long-term leases which require periodic payments similar to interest expense. Lease expense is added to both the numerator and denominator of the number of times interest earned ratio. The fixed charge coverage ratio can be calculated as follows:

$$\text{Fixed Charge Coverage Ratio} = \frac{\text{Income Before Income Taxes} + \text{Interest Expense} + \text{Lease Expense}}{\text{Interest Expense} + \text{Lease Expense}}$$

Activity Ratios

It is management's responsibility to generate earnings for owners while providing products and services to guests. Activity ratios measure the effectiveness with which management uses the resources of the property.

Inventory Turnover

This ratio measures the number of times inventory turns over during the period. Generally, the greater the number of times the better, because inventories can be expensive to maintain. Inventory turnovers are usually calculated separately for food items and beverage items. To calculate inventory turnover it is first necessary to determine the average inventory. This is accomplished by adding inventory at the beginning and end of the period and then dividing that figure by two. The food inventory turnover can be calculated as follows:

$$\text{Food Inventory Turnover} = \frac{\text{Cost of Food Used}}{\text{Average Food Inventory}}$$

Fixed Assets Turnover

This ratio measures management's effectiveness in using the property's fixed assets. A high turnover suggests that the property's fixed assets are being used effectively to generate revenue; a low turnover suggests that the property is not making effective use of its fixed assets. The fixed assets turnover is calculated by dividing average total fixed assets into total revenue for the period. To calculate the fixed assets turnover it is first necessary to determine the average total fixed assets. This is accomplished by totaling fixed assets at the beginning and end of the period and then dividing that figure by two. The fixed assets turnover can be calculated as follows:

$$\text{Fixed Assets Turnover} = \frac{\text{Total Revenue}}{\text{Average Total Fixed Assets}}$$

Profitability Ratios

Profitability ratios reflect the overall effectiveness of management in producing the bottom line figure expected by owners and creditors. Owners invest in lodging properties in order to increase their wealth through dividends and through increases in the price of the property's capital stock. Dividends and stock prices are highly dependent upon the profits generated by the operation. Since future profits may be required to repay lenders, creditors normally perceive less risk to be involved in dealings with the more profitable businesses in their communities.

Profit Margin Ratio

This ratio measures management's overall ability to produce profits by generating sales and controlling expenses. The profit margin ratio is calculated by dividing net income by total revenue. The net income figure represents income after *all* expenses have been deducted—expenses controllable by management and expenses directly related to decisions made by the property's owners. The profit margin ratio can be calculated as follows:

$$\text{Profit Margin Ratio} \ = \ \frac{\text{Net Income}}{\text{Total Revenue}}$$

Return on Owners' Equity Ratio

This ratio measures the profitability of the lodging property by comparing the profits of the property to the owners' investment. The return on owners' equity ratio is calculated by dividing net income by average owners' equity. To calculate this ratio it is first necessary to determine the average owners' equity for the period. This is accomplished by totaling owners' equity at the beginning and end of the period and then dividing that figure by two. The return on owners' equity ratio can be calculated as follows:

$$\text{Return on Owners' Equity Ratio} \ = \ \frac{\text{Net Income}}{\text{Average Owners' Equity}}$$

Return on Assets Ratio

This ratio is a general indicator of the profitability of the operation and is calculated by dividing net income by the average total assets. To calculate the return on assets ratio it is first necessary to determine the average total assets. This is accomplished by totaling assets at the beginning and end of the period and then dividing that figure by two. The return on assets ratio can be calculated as follows:

$$\text{Return on Assets Ratio} \ = \ \frac{\text{Net Income}}{\text{Average Total Assets}}$$

Return on Fixed Assets Ratio

This ratio measures the profitability of a hotel or motel by comparing net income to average total fixed assets. The return on fixed assets ratio is calculated by dividing net income by the average total fixed assets. To calculate the return on fixed assets ratio it is first necessary to determine the average total fixed assets. This is accomplished by totaling fixed assets at the beginning and end of the period and then dividing that figure by two. The return on fixed assets ratio can be calculated as follows:

$$\text{Return on Fixed Assets Ratio} = \frac{\text{Net Income}}{\text{Average Total Fixed Assets}}$$

Operating Ratios

Operating ratios assist management in analyzing the operations of the lodging property. These ratios relate expenses to revenue and are useful for control purposes when the ratio results are compared to budgeted or planned ratio goals. Significant variations between actual ratio results and budgeted or planned goals may indicate the need for further analysis and corrective action by management.

Average Room Rate

Although room rates may vary within a property, many lodging property managers calculate an average room rate. The average room rate reveals the average rate charged per paid room occupied and is calculated by dividing rooms revenue by the number of paid rooms occupied. Paid rooms occupied are rooms occupied by lodging property guests on a paid basis. The average room rate can be calculated as follows:

$$\text{Average Room Rate} = \frac{\text{Rooms Revenue}}{\text{Paid Rooms Occupied}}$$

Average Food Check

This operating ratio reveals the amount of the average food check per cover and is calculated by dividing total food revenue by the number of covers. Covers refers to guests served in the food operation during the period. The average food check can be calculated as follows:

$$\text{Average Food Check} = \frac{\text{Total Food Revenue}}{\text{Number of Covers}}$$

Food Cost Percentage

This operating ratio compares the cost of food sales to food revenue. Many food service managers rely heavily on this ratio in determining whether food costs are reasonable. Food cost percentage is calculated by dividing the cost of food sales by food revenue. The food cost percentage can be calculated as follows:

$$\text{Food Cost Percentage} = \frac{\text{Cost of Food Sales}}{\text{Food Revenue}}$$

Labor Cost Percentage

The largest expense for most lodging properties is labor. Labor expense includes total payroll and related expenses for all departments and operational areas of the property. A general labor cost percentage is calculated by dividing total payroll and related expenses by total revenue. This general labor cost percentage is simply a benchmark for making broad comparisons. For control purposes, labor cost percentages should be calculated and analyzed for each department and operational area of the property. The labor cost percentage can be calculated as follows:

$$\text{Labor Cost Percentage} = \frac{\text{Payroll and Related Expenses}}{\text{Total Revenue}}$$

ROOM STATISTICS AND OCCUPANCY RATIOS

Full-service and limited-service lodging properties usually supplement the rooms operation information reported on the Statement of Income with occupancy ratio results. Occupancy ratios measure the success of the rooms operation in selling the primary product of the property. In order to calculate basic occupancy ratios, various rooms statistics must be kept during the period. The following is a list with definitions of several common rooms statistics and occupancy ratios.

(1)	Number of Rooms in Hotel	
(2)	Less: Permanent House Use	_____
(3)	Rooms Available	=======
	Number of Paid Rooms Occupied:	
(4)	Transient: Regular	
(5)	Transient: Group	
(6)	Permanent	_____
(7)	Paid Rooms Occupied	
(8)	Number of Complimentary Rooms	_____
(9)	Rooms Occupied by Guests	
(10)	Temporary House Use Rooms	_____
(11)	Rooms in Use	
(12)	Number of Rooms Vacant	_____
(13)	Rooms Available for Sale	
(14)	Rooms Out-of-Order	_____
(15)	Rooms Available	=======
	Percentage of Occupancy:	
(16)	Transient: Regular %	
(17)	Transient: Group %	
(18)	Permanent %	
(19)	Paid Occupancy %	
(20)	Complimentary Rooms %	
(21)	Guest Occupancy %	
(22)	Temporary House Use %	
(23)	Total Occupancy %	
	Average Daily Rate:	
(24)	Transient: Regular	
(25)	Transient: Group	
(26)	Permanent	
(27)	Overall	
	Number of Guests:	
(28)	Transient: Regular	
(29)	Transient: Group	
(30)	Permanent	_____
(31)	Paid Guests	

(32)   Complimentary Guests
(33)   Total Guests
(34)   Number of Guests per Occupied Room
(35)   Number of Rooms with Multiple Guests
(36)   Multiple Occupancy %
(37)   Arrivals
(38)   Average Length of Stay
(39)   Revenue per Available Room (REVPAR)
(40)   Cost per Occupied Room

Other relevant statistics include payroll and other expenses per occupied room and/ or per guest and as a percentage of revenue.

DEFINITIONS:

(1)   **Number of Rooms in Hotel**
Total number of guestrooms in the hotel.

(2)   **Permanent House Use**
Those guestrooms removed from salable inventory for an extended period of time.

(3)   **Rooms Available**
(1) Number of Rooms in Hotel, less (2) Permanent House Use.

(7)   **Paid Rooms Occupied**
Rooms occupied by hotel guests on a paid basis for each market segment: (4) Transient: Regular, (5) Transient: Group, (6) Permanent and, if significant, Transient: Contract.

(8)   **Complimentary Rooms**
Those rooms occupied by hotel guests on a gratis basis.

(9)   **Rooms Occupied by Guests**
Total of (7) Paid Rooms Occupied and (8) Complimentary Rooms.

(10)   **Temporary House Use Rooms**
Those rooms taken out of inventory on a short-term basis.

(11)   **Rooms In Use**
Total of (9) Rooms Occupied by Guests and (10) Temporary House Use Rooms.

(12)   **Rooms Vacant**
Those salable guestrooms that were not occupied during the period.

(13)   **Rooms Available for Sale**
Total (11) Rooms In Use and (12) Rooms Vacant.

(14)   **Rooms Out-of-Order**
Those rooms removed from salable inventory due to renovation or a temporary fault or problem rendering them inadequate for occupancy.

(15)   **Rooms Available**
Total (13) Rooms Available for Sale and (14) Rooms Out-of-Order.

FORMULAS
Percentage of Occupancy:

$$(16) \quad \text{Transient: Regular} = \frac{(4) \quad \begin{array}{c}\text{Number of Paid Rooms Occupied:}\\ \text{Transient: Regular}\end{array}}{(3) \quad \text{Rooms Available}} \times 100$$

$$(17) \quad \text{Transient: Group} = \frac{(5) \quad \begin{array}{c}\text{Number of Paid Rooms Occupied:}\\ \text{Transient: Group}\end{array}}{(3) \quad \text{Rooms Available}} \times 100$$

$$(18) \quad \text{Permanent} = \frac{(6) \quad \begin{array}{c}\text{Number of Paid Rooms Occupied:}\\ \text{Permanent}\end{array}}{(3) \quad \text{Rooms Available}} \times 100$$

$$(19) \quad \text{Paid Occupancy} = \frac{(7) \quad \text{Paid Rooms Occupied}}{(3) \quad \text{Rooms Available}} \times 100$$

$$(20) \quad \text{Complimentary} = \frac{(8) \quad \text{Complimentary Rooms}}{(3) \quad \text{Rooms Available}} \times 100$$

$$(21) \quad \text{Guest Occupancy} = \frac{(9) \quad \text{Rooms Occupied by Guests}}{(3) \quad \text{Rooms Available}} \times 100$$

$$(22) \quad \text{Temporary House Use} = \frac{(10) \quad \text{Temporary House Use Rooms}}{(3) \quad \text{Rooms Available}} \times 100$$

$$(23) \quad \text{Total Occupancy} = \frac{(11) \quad \text{Rooms in Use}}{(3) \quad \text{Rooms Available}} \times 100$$

Average Daily Rate:

$$(24) \quad \text{Transient: Regular} = \frac{\begin{array}{c}\text{Revenue: Transient: Regular less}\\ \text{Transient: Regular Allowances}\end{array}}{(4) \quad \begin{array}{c}\text{Number of Paid Rooms Occupied}\\ \text{Transient: Regular}\end{array}}$$

$$(25) \quad \text{Transient: Group} = \frac{\begin{array}{c}\text{Revenue: Transient: Group less}\\ \text{Transient: Group Allowances}\end{array}}{(5) \quad \begin{array}{c}\text{Number of Paid Rooms Occupied}\\ \text{Transient: Group}\end{array}}$$

$$(26) \quad \text{Permanent} = \frac{\begin{array}{c}\text{Revenue: Permanent less}\\ \text{Permanent Allowances}\end{array}}{(6) \quad \begin{array}{c}\text{Number of Paid Rooms Occupied}\\ \text{Permanent}\end{array}}$$

(27) Overall $= \dfrac{\text{Net Revenue}}{(7) \quad \text{Paid Rooms Occupied}}$

(If Transient: Contract Rooms is a significant portion of the hotel's business, a separate Average Daily Rate should be determined.)

Number of Guests: Number of registered guests in each category of occupied rooms.

(34) Number of Guests per Occupied Room $= \dfrac{(33) \quad \text{Total Guests}}{(9) \quad \text{Rooms Occupied by Guests}}$

(35) Number of Rooms with Multiple Guests: Number of rooms occupied by two or more registered guests.

(36) Multiple Occupancy % $= \dfrac{(35) \quad \text{Number of Rooms with Multiple Guests}}{(9) \quad \text{Rooms Occupied by Guests}} \times 100$

(37) Arrivals: Number of guest check-ins for the period.

(38) Average Length of Stay: Represents the average number of days of a guest's stay.

$= \dfrac{(33) \quad \text{Total Guests}}{(37) \quad \text{Arrivals}}$

(39) Revenue Per Available Room $= \dfrac{\text{Total Rooms Revenues}}{(13) \quad \text{Rooms Available for Sale}}$

(40) Cost per Occupied Room $= \dfrac{\text{Total Rooms Department Cost}}{(9) \quad \text{Rooms Occupied by Guests}}$

FOOD AND BEVERAGE STATISTICS

The following indicates the kind of food and beverage statistical information that the financial report of hotels should contain:

Restaurant Facilities

Number of Seats
Meal Period Statistics

Meal Period	Covers	Average Check
Breakfast		
Lunch		
Dinner		
Total		

Beverage sales % of food sales
Combined food and beverage sales per seat

Lounge Facilities

Number of Seats
Sales per Seat

Room Service

Total Sales per Occupied Room

Banquet

Total Square Feet
Banquet Sales per Square Foot
Covers and Average Check Statistics (See *Restaurant Facilities*)

Inventory Turns and Number of Days of Inventory on Hand

These inventory statistics are calculated as follows for both food and beverage inventories:

Inventory Turns

Monthly Cost of Goods Consumed divided by Average Inventory (Opening Inventory plus Closing Inventory divided by two).

Number of Days of Inventory on Hand

Number of days in the month divided by the inventory turns equals the average number of days it takes to turn the inventory over.

Section 11
Breakeven Analysis

The breakeven point of a lodging operation is the level of revenue at which the property's total revenue equals total costs. Although most properties desire to do much better than just break even financially, breakeven analysis serves as a reference point for managers planning operations for the period. The breakeven point can be illustrated by the following graph:

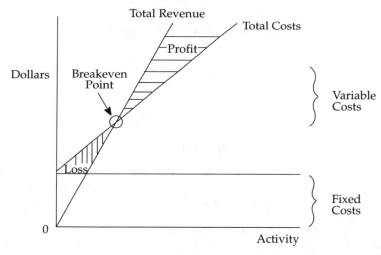

The graph shows that profit (net income) is zero at the breakeven point. The difference between the total revenue and total cost lines to the right of the breakeven point represents profit. The difference between the total revenue and total cost lines to the left of the breakeven point represents loss. A formula for determining the breakeven point is as follows:

$$\text{Breakeven Point} = \frac{\text{Fixed Costs}}{\text{Contribution Margin Percentage}}$$

To calculate the breakeven point, it is first necessary to determine fixed costs and the contribution margin percentage.

Fixed, Variable, and Mixed Costs

Lodging operations incur three basic kinds of costs: fixed, variable, and mixed. Fixed costs are costs that remain constant in the short run, even though sales volume varies. Common examples of fixed costs include: salaries, rent expense, insurance expense, property taxes, depreciation expense, and interest expense. Variable costs are costs that change proportionately with the volume of sales activity. For example, if the number of steak dinners increases by ten percent, the cost of food sold for those dinners may be expected to increase by ten percent. Mixed costs are costs composed of fixed and variable elements. An example of a mixed cost is telecommunications expense. Telecommunications expense is mixed because, although the basic cost of the system is fixed, variable costs arise in terms of usage rates that coincide with increases or decreases in activity.

In order to calculate the breakeven point, mixed costs must be divided into their fixed and variable elements. Three methods for determining the elements of a mixed cost are: the high/low two-point method, the scatter diagram, and regression analysis. Detailed explanations of these methods are beyond the scope of this book. Interested readers are referred to *Hospitality Industry Managerial Accounting*, 3d Edition, by Raymond S. Schmidgall and published by the Educational Institute of the American Hotel & Motel Association.

Contribution Margin Percentage

The contribution margin percentage is the percentage of each revenue dollar that is available to cover fixed costs. A formula for determining the contribution margin percentage follows:

$$\text{Contribution Margin Percentage} = \frac{\text{Total Revenue} - \text{Variable Costs}}{\text{Total Revenue}}$$

Illustration

As an example, consider the sample Summary Statement of Income shown on the next page. To simplify the illustration, assume that all operated department expenses are variable costs and that all undistributed operating expenses, rent, property taxes, insurance, interest, and depreciation expenses are fixed costs.

The first step is to calculate the contribution margin percentage. This is accomplished by subtracting the variable costs (the expenses of the operated departments in this example) from total revenue and then dividing that figure by total revenue:

$$\text{Contribution Margin Percentage} = \frac{\$180,000 - \$103,000}{\$180,000}$$

$$= \frac{\$77,000}{\$180,000}$$

$$= \underline{.4278} \text{ or } 42.78\%$$

This figure reveals that, after covering variable costs, 42.78% of each revenue dollar is available to cover fixed costs.

The second step is to calculate the breakeven point by dividing fixed costs by the contribution margin percentage. Since for the purposes of our illustration the fixed costs include the sum of the undistributed operating expenses and fixed charges, the breakeven point can be calculated as follows:

$$\text{Breakeven Point} = \frac{\$47,000 + \$7,000 + \$5,000 + \$10,000}{.4278}$$

$$= \frac{\$69,000}{.4278}$$

$$= \underline{\$161,290.32}$$

This figure reveals that the property in this example needs $161,290.32 in total revenue in order to break even. These calculations ignore the gain on sale of property because this is a nonoperating activity. Also, income taxes are ignored because at the breakeven point they are assumed to be zero.

Revenues required to achieve various profit levels can be determined using modifications of breakeven analysis. Interested readers should consider the *Hospitality Industry Managerial Accounting* book for more details.

Sample Summary Statement of Income

	Revenue	Cost of Sales	Payroll and Related Expenses	Other Expenses	Income (Loss)
OPERATED DEPARTMENTS					
Rooms	$ 120,000	$ 0	$ 30,000	$ 30,000	$ 60,000
Food	50,000	20,000	15,000	8,000	7,000
Rentals and Other Income	10,000	0	0	0	10,000
Total Operated Departments	180,000	20,000	45,000	38,000	77,000
UNDISTRIBUTED OPERATING EXPENSES					
Administrative and General			20,000	2,000	22,000
Marketing			0	5,000	5,000
Property Operation and Maintenance			5,000	3,000	8,000
Utility Costs			0	12,000	12,000
Total Undistributed Operating Expenses			25,000	22,000	47,000
Totals	$ 180,000	$ 20,000	$ 70,000	$ 60,000	
INCOME AFTER UNDISTRIBUTED OPERATING EXPENSES					30,000
Rent, Property Taxes, and Insurance					7,000
Interest Expense					5,000
Depreciation Expense					10,000
Gain on Sale of Property					2,000
INCOME BEFORE INCOME TAXES					10,000
Income Taxes					3,000
NET INCOME					$ 7,000

Section 12
Operations Budgeting
and Budgetary Control

The annual operations budget is a profit plan for the property which addresses all revenue sources and expense items appearing on the Summary Statement of Income and related supplemental schedules. Annual budgets are the summation of twelve monthly plans. These monthly plans form the basis against which management should evaluate the actual results of operations. Thus, the operations budget enables management to accomplish two of its most important functions: planning and control.

Preparing the Operations Budget

The budget process requires a closely coordinated effort of all supervisory and management personnel. Each manager responsible for a department or an activity within the property should participate in the process. When managers are given real input into the budget process, they often become more motivated to implement the property's profit plan and are less likely to attribute off-plan performance to unrealistic plans.

The accounting department normally supplies managers with statistical information on previous performance, labor costs, maintenance program status, and other data essential to the budget preparation process. The financial controller generally is responsible for coordinating the budget plans of individual department managers. The accounting department compiles these plans into a comprehensive operations budget, including fixed charges and other expenses, for the general manager's review and approval.

The general manager and the controller review the departmental budget plans and prepare the General Manager's Budget Report for approval by the property's owners. If the budget is not satisfactory, elements requiring change are returned to the appropriate department managers for review and revision.

To ensure that adequate time is available for preparing the operations budget and securing its approval, a time schedule should be set and closely followed. Properties whose fiscal year coincides with the calendar year may consider something like the following time schedule:

WHO	WHAT	WHEN
General Manager	Budget Planning Meetings	October 1–31
Controller Department Heads	Preparation of Departmental Budget Plans	November 1–9
Accounting	Consolidation of Departmental Budget Plans	November 10–19
General Manager Controller	Preparation of the General Manager's Budget Report	December
Owners	Review and Approval of the General Manager's Budget Report	December

The following sections present a detailed explanation of each step in the budget preparation process.

Budget Planning Meetings

At budget planning meetings, direction is provided for department heads to prepare detailed departmental budget proposals. An overall plan for these meetings and specific agendas for each meeting ensure the most effective and efficient use of everyone's time. A possible sequence of tasks to be accomplished at budget planning meetings is as follows:

- Review the current year's operations.
- Analyze general business conditions.
- Analyze the current competitive situation.
- Analyze rates.
- Project occupancy levels and gross sales.

The following sections discuss each of these tasks which may be accomplished at budget planning meetings.

- *Review the current year's operations.* A review of property operations for the current year identifies items of *continuing significance.* These may include rate changes, additions to facilities or reductions in existing facilities, major labor changes, improvements in efficiency that were implemented during the year, and other similar items. The principal causes of any failures or successes in meeting the current year's budgeted results are thoroughly discussed. The potential effect of such items on property operations for the upcoming year is projected so that the budget being prepared is based upon the proper revenue and cost statistics.

- *Analyze general business conditions.* An analysis of current national and local economic and political conditions identifies items that may significantly affect operations for the upcoming year. An analysis of political conditions may reveal new legislative proposals and/or scheduled legislative changes concerning, for example, wage rates and payroll taxes. The potential effect of such items on property operations for the upcoming year is projected and then reflected in the budget being prepared. Also, action plans are developed to either capitalize upon favorable economic and political conditions or offset unfavorable conditions. The potential effect of these action plans on property operations is projected and, if necessary, reflected in the budget being prepared.

- *Analyze the current competitive situation.* An analysis of the current competitive situation identifies items that may significantly affect operations for the upcoming year. Examples of such items include newly constructed hotels, motels, and restaurants and/or major renovations to existing properties. A full-service property commonly analyzes the competitive situation in relation to *each area* of service the property offers. The potential effect of such items on property operations for the upcoming year is projected and then reflected in the budget being prepared. Also, action plans are developed to either capitalize upon favorable competitive situations or offset unfavorable situations. The potential effect of these action plans on property operations is projected and, if necessary, reflected in the budget being prepared.

- *Analyze rates.* An analysis of the rate structure for all products and services offered by the property examines rates that will attract the volume of business necessary to best utilize the property's facilities. This analysis focuses on maximizing revenue by establishing the maximum rates possible while avoiding a major reduction in volume. During this analysis, *each rate category in each department* of the property is reviewed and a determination made regarding its adequacy and/or need for change within the upcoming year. If a rate change is indicated, further analysis is undertaken to determine the specific changes (i.e., which rooms should be changed and by how much, which meals and by how much, etc.) and the time it will take to implement the changes (including lead time). When rate changes are approved, they should be implemented as soon as possible to ensure that the property benefits from them quickly.

- *Project occupancy levels and gross sales.* Occupancy projections for each month of the upcoming year are estimated for each market source listed on the Summary Statement of Income or the rooms department schedule. These sources may include transient—regular, transient—group, permanent residents, or other market sources. Occupancy projections are generally made on the basis of historical data, reservations, and statistical information on group business. Gross sales projections are made for banquet and regular business of food and beverage facilities. Banquet projections are generally made on the basis of catering records; projections for regular business are made on the basis of past sales records. Projections for other revenue-producing departments (i.e., telecommunications, gift shop, garage and parking, etc.) are based upon occupancy projections and other relevant information. These projections of occupancy and gross sales enable the general manager to estimate the total gross revenue for the upcoming year.

Preparation of Departmental Budget Plans

Using information made available at the budget planning meetings and month-by-month comparisons of the current year's operational results and the current year's operational budget, department heads project the monthly sales volume of their areas of responsibility for the upcoming year. Departmental revenue can then be estimated on the basis of volume figures and rate schedules agreed upon at the budget planning meetings.

After estimating sales volume and revenue, department heads project the costs of sales and operating expenses. The accounting department provides each department head with basic information for projecting costs. This information generally includes a salary schedule, fringe benefit changes, anticipated contract changes, price index (general cost changes), and known tax increases. Managers should also review the progress of the current year, especially monthly reports that compare current costs of sales and operating expenses to budgeted figures of the current year's profit plan.

Departmental budget plans are commonly supported by detailed information gathered in the budget preparation process and recorded on worksheets and summary sheets. These documents should be saved to provide a record of the reasoning behind decisions made while preparing departmental budget plans. Such records may answer questions that arise during budget review stages. These documents may also provide valuable assistance in the preparation of future years' budgets.

To prevent delays in the review stages of the budget process, department heads should submit with their budget plans detailed information describing any extraordinary charges to operations, such as unusual maintenance and repair expenses or changes in classifications of service. Those department heads whose budget plans call for extraordinary charges to operations must justify the charges, and the group must identify the effects of such charges on operations during the upcoming year. After discussion, the general manager is responsible for determining which requests can be granted, which requests must be deferred until a later date, and which requests will require the borrowing of money. Finally, the potential effect of requests granted for the upcoming year is projected and then reflected in the budget being prepared.

Consolidation of Departmental Budget Plans

The completed departmental budget plans are forwarded to the accounting department where they are reviewed for accuracy and completeness. The accounting department is also responsible for ensuring that all forms and schedules accompanying the departmental budget plans are complete.

After completing a review of the departmental budget plans, the accounting department prepares a projected Summary Statement of Income for the upcoming year. This statement, along with departmental schedules and supporting data, becomes the total preliminary budget package to be reviewed by the property's general manager and controller. This preliminary budget package should also include any pertinent information discovered by the accounting department while consolidating the departmental budget plans.

Preparation of the General Manager's Budget Report

The general manager and the controller review the Summary Statement of Income, departmental schedules, and supporting data to ensure that all items are reasonable and that revenue and expense goals are realistic. This review also coordinates the budget plans of all departments, ensuring that the plan of operations for each department is fully recognized and reflected in the plans of the other departments.

Earnings indicated by the Summary Statement of Income are measured against the general manager's projection of the property's earning potential. If additional adjustments to departmental budgets are required, the general manager and controller meet with the appropriate managers to identify how they will be made. If major adjustments are made, the effects of such changes on the budgets of other departments and/or the total budget package are carefully analyzed.

The General Manager's Budget Report also includes important information which arose during the budget planning meetings. The report generally includes a review of the following items:

- Competition
- Economic and political conditions
- Proposed changes in operations
- Extraordinary items
- Personnel
- Facilities
- Rates
- Capital improvements
- Cash flow

Before submitting the General Manager's Budget Report for approval and adoption by the owners, the general manager and the controller should briefly review the report with department heads.

Review and Approval of the General Manager's Budget Report

After reviewing the final budget report with department heads, the general manager and the controller present the operations budget to the owners of the property. If the budget is not satisfactory, elements requiring change are returned to the appropriate department managers for review and revision. This process may be repeated several times until a satisfactory budget is prepared.

Budgetary Control

The process of budgetary control identifies and analyzes significant variances between budgeted amounts and actual results of operations. Variance analysis may indicate that additional investigation by management is required to determine the exact causes of significant variances. Once these causes have been identified, management is able to take necessary corrective actions.

In order for budgets to be used effectively for control purposes, reports are generally prepared on a monthly basis. These reports are useful only when they are timely and relevant. Reports issued weeks after the end of an accounting period are too late to allow managers to investigate variances, determine causes, and take necessary corrective actions. Relevant reports include only the revenue and expenses for which the individual department heads are responsible. From a control perspective, for example, it is relatively meaningless to include allocated administrative and general salaries on a rooms department report because the rooms department manager is unable to take any action to affect these allocated costs.

Reports should include sufficient detail to allow department heads to make reasonable judgments regarding variances from the budget plan. Almost all budgeted revenue and expense items on the report will differ from actual results of operations. This is to be expected because no budgeting process is perfect. However, simply because a variance exists does not mean that management should analyze it and follow through with appropriate corrective actions. Only significant variances require this kind of management analysis and action.

The general manager and controller should provide department heads with criteria by which to determine significant variances. When such criteria are expressed in terms of dollar and percentage differences, the format of the monthly reports should include dollar and percentage variances columns so that department heads can easily identify which variances are significant. Two sample budget report formats are provided in Section 9 covering financial statement formats; however, each property should design the format of its monthly report to meet its own particular needs and requirements.

Variance analysis is beyond the scope of this book; however, interested readers are referred to *Hospitality Industry Managerial Accounting,* 3rd Edition, published by the Educational Institute of the American Hotel & Motel Association.

Reforecasting

Many properties reforecast expected results of operations and revise operations budgets as they progress through the budget year. This reforecasting is necessary only when actual results begin to vary significantly from the operations budget because of changes that occur after the budget has been prepared.

Section 13
Guidelines for Allocating Expenses to Operated Departments (Responsibility Accounting)

The department income of the revenue departments (e.g., rooms, food, and beverage) is computed by charging against revenues only a limited number of expenses that are traceable to the department. For instance, undistributed operating expenses, such as marketing and property operation and maintenance, and expenses that are charged against gross operating profit such as rent, insurance, depreciation, and property taxes are not charged against revenue departments. This measurement approach to departmental income is chosen to help ensure account uniformity. Uniformity is important for the comparability of operating units.

Because of this approach to departmental income measurement, departmental expenses omit a number of significant costs that may be incurred by a revenue department. It may be necessary to ascribe many of the undistributed operating expenses and deductions from gross operating profit to the revenue departments to have a complete measure of departmental performance. There may be times when managers wish to know the overall cost of operating a department. This information is useful for assessing the profitability of a department, for determining prices for services and goods, and for considering whether outsourcing for the services is practicable. Identifying the costs incurred by a department is also useful for making managers responsible for the consumption of resources that leads to cost incurrence. Managers who are charged for resources may consume them more judiciously than those who do not feel responsible for certain costs. Charging costs to revenue departments may also provide departmental managers with more incentive to monitor the costs of service departments, since these costs are going to be assigned to their departments.

If assigning these costs is deemed to be valuable to management for decision making, efforts to determine a reasonable and fair basis for assigning costs are encouraged. The cost assignment, however, should be supplementary to the presentation of the departmental results after they have been stated in accordance with the *Uniform System of Accounts for the Lodging Industry.* The basis for the assigning of costs to revenue departments will vary by operating unit. Any approach to cost assignment undertaken should use a systematic and logical approach that reflects resource consumption. One approach would be to group undistributed expenses into two categories:

1. Those that are directly traceable to profit centers.
2. Those that need to be allocated to departments based on resources consumed.

For instance, if maintenance and repair expenses or rent expense can be traced directly to a profit center, then these costs can be assigned to that department without having to make any assumption about cost behavior. If costs cannot be directly traced, an apportionment can be undertaken by allocating costs among the departments using a reasonable allocation base. However, managers should apportion only those costs that management believes could be avoided if the department or departments were to be discontinued.

	Rooms	Food	Beverage	Other
Revenue Department—Schedule of Profit or Loss				
NET REVENUE				
EXPENSES				
REPORTED DEPARTMENTAL INCOME				
LESS:				
Traceable Undistributed Expenses				
Traceable Departmental Income				
LESS:				
Allocated Undistributed Expenses				
Adjusted Departmental Income				

Allocation When There Are Multiple Service Departments

The requirements of an allocation are:

a. An appropriate accounting system, such as that described by the *Uniform System of Accounts for the Lodging Industry.*

b. Adequate statistical information for development of the allocation bases.

Many times, lodging properties have a number of service departments. Managers may wish to allocate the costs of these departments to revenue departments. Because service departments provide resources to other service departments as well as to revenue departments, the allocation of these costs requires some systematic allocation process. Three approaches currently used in practice are:

1. The direct method. All undistributed expenses are charged directly to the revenue departments on some logical basis such as percentage of total revenue, departmental payroll, or square feet of area.

2. The step method. Undistributed expenses from a service department are allocated to both revenue departments and other service departments. Under this procedure, one department is selected for allocation first, and the expenses are apportioned on some logical basis. The remaining departments are allocated similarly.

3. The formula method, by which allocation of each department is made simultaneously to all other departments serviced by that department, whether or not they are revenue departments. Under this method, the overhead departments are classified as those that service each other as well as revenue departments, and those that service only revenue departments. Those serving

overhead as well as revenue departments are allocated first, but the entire process is generally performed by a computer.

Although any of the accepted methods will provide useful information if followed consistently, the formula method produces results that more nearly reflect the interdepartmental activities. Under any method, the following steps are required:

1. Collect the data, including interdepartmental services and other information required for determining the basis for allocation.

2. Reclassify, if necessary. For example, some allocations may be made each month on a routine basis. These may need to be reversed in order for the apportionment of expenses to be more precise.

3. Allocate rent, taxes, and insurance to all departments on a direct basis.

4. Allocate the remaining departments, including their share of fixed costs, using one of the accepted methods.

Part III
Recording Financial Information

Section 14
Sample Chart of Accounts

The following pages present a sample chart of accounts which is intended to be used only as a guide to establishing an accounting system for recording business transactions. It is designed to be broad enough to have a major number for each account that is regularly used in standard reporting, and sufficiently detailed to provide sub-accounts for all departments or areas of significance.

The sample chart of accounts uses a twelve-digit numbering system, consisting of four clusters of three digits each. The clusters are defined as follows:

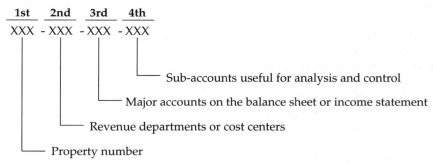

1st	2nd	3rd	4th

XXX - XXX - XXX - XXX

      Sub-accounts useful for analysis and control

    Major accounts on the balance sheet or income statement

   Revenue departments or cost centers

  Property number

No attempt has been made to meet the specific needs of every property. The chart of accounts presented here is sufficiently flexible to allow companies, individual owners, or managers to add or delete accounts to meet the needs and requirements of their properties. For example, a single property owner/operator may choose to eliminate the first and fourth clusters, using only the second cluster to represent departments and the third cluster to indicate the major general ledger accounts.

As another example, one company might define Cash as account number 100 within the third cluster and use the fourth cluster to indicate individual banks (First National, City Savings and Trust, etc.), while another company might use the fourth cluster to indicate the type of account, such as House Funds, Checking Account, or Payroll Account. It is also possible to use the third and fourth cluster to indicate both the individual bank and the type of account.

Since it is more likely that smaller properties might find a suggested chart of accounts useful, the following is provided for that purpose. Only the second and third cluster are used.

The suggestions for assigning the digits within the second cluster (revenue department or cost center) are:

000 The whole lodging property; no specific department

100 Rooms Department as an entity; possible subdivisions include:

120 Front Office
140 Reservations
160 Housekeeping
180 Uniform Service
200 Food Department as an entity; possible subdivisions include:
210 Coffee Shop
220 Specialty/Fine Dining Room
230 Banquet Department
240 Room Service
270 Kitchen
290 Employee Cafeteria
300 Beverage Department as an entity; possible subdivisions include:
310 Bar/Lounge
320 Banquet Department
400 Telecommunications Department
500 Gift Shop
550 Garage and Parking
570 Other Operated Departments
590 Rentals and Other Income
600 Administrative and General as an entity; possible subdivisions include:
610 Accounting
620 Data Processing
640 Human Resources
650 Purchasing
670 Security
690 Transportation
700 Marketing
800 Property Operation and Maintenance
850 Utility Costs
900 Management Fees
950 Fixed Charges

Suggestions for assigning the digits within the third cluster (major accounts) are:

100–199 Assets
200–279 Liabilities
280–299 Equity
300–399 Revenue
400–499 Cost of Sales
500–599 Payroll
600–699 Other Expenses
700–799 Fixed Charges

The following pages provide a more detailed assignment of the major account numbers.

ASSETS

100 Cash
    101 House Funds
    103 Checking Account
    105 Payroll Account
    107 Savings Account
    109 Petty Cash
110 Short-Term Investments
120 Accounts Receivable
    121 Guest Ledger
    122 Credit Card Accounts
    123 Direct Bill
    124 Notes Receivable (Current)
    125 Due from Employees
    126 Receivable from Owner
    127 Other Accounts Receivable
    128 Intercompany Receivables
    129 Allowance for Doubtful Accounts
130 Inventory
    131 Food
    132 Liquor
    133 Wine
    135 Operating Supplies
    136 Paper Supplies
    137 Cleaning Supplies
    138 China, Glassware, Silver, Linen, and Uniforms (Unopened Stock)
    139 Other
140 Prepaids
    141 Prepaid Insurance
    142 Prepaid Taxes
    143 Prepaid Workers' Compensation
    144 Prepaid Supplies
    145 Prepaid Contracts
    146 Current Deferred Tax Asset
    147 Barter Contracts Asset
    149 Other Prepaids
150 Noncurrent Receivables
155 Investments (not short-term)
160 Property and Equipment
    161 Land
    162 Buildings
    163 Accumulated Depreciation—Buildings
    164 Leaseholds and Leasehold Improvements
    165 Accumulated Depreciation—Leaseholds
    166 Furniture and Fixtures
    167 Accumulated Depreciation—Furniture and Fixtures

168 Machinery and Equipment
169 Accumulated Depreciation—Machinery and Equipment
170 Information Systems Equipment
171 Accumulated Depreciation—Information Systems Equipment
172 Automobiles and Trucks
173 Accumulated Depreciation—Automobiles and Trucks
174 Construction in Progress
175 China
176 Glassware
177 Silver
178 Linen
179 Uniforms
180 Accumulated Depreciation—China, Glassware, Silver, Linen, and Uniforms
190 Other Assets
191 Security Deposits
192 Deferred Charges
193 Long-Term Deferred Tax Asset
196 Cash Surrender Value—Life Insurance
197 Goodwill
199 Miscellaneous

LIABILITIES

200 Payables
201 Accounts Payable
205 Dividends Payable
207 Notes Payable
209 Intercompany Payables
210 Employee Withholdings
211 FICA—Employee
212 State Disability—Employee
213 SUTA—Employee
214 Medical Insurance—Employee
215 Life Insurance—Employee
216 Dental Insurance—Employee
217 Credit Union
218 United Way
219 Miscellaneous Deductions
220 Employer Payroll Taxes
221 FICA—Employer
222 FUTA—Employer
223 SUTA—Employer
224 Medical Insurance—Employer
225 Life Insurance—Employer
226 Dental Insurance—Employer
227 Disability—Employer

228 Workers' Compensation—Employer
229 Miscellaneous Contributions
230 Taxes
  231 Federal Withholding Tax
  232 State Withholding Tax
  233 County Withholding Tax
  234 City Withholding Tax
  236 Sales Tax
  238 Property Tax
  241 Federal Income Tax
  242 State Income Tax
  244 City Income Tax
255 Advance Deposits
260 Accruals
  261 Accrued Payables
  262 Accrued Utilities
  263 Accrued Vacation
  264 Accrued Taxes
  267 Barter Contracts Liability
  269 Accrued Expenses—Other
270 Current Portion—Long-Term Debt
272 Other Current Liabilities
273 Current Deferred Tax Liability
275 Long-Term Debt
276 Capital Leases
277 Other Long-Term Debt
278 Long-Term Deferred Tax Liability

EQUITY

For Proprietorships and Partnerships:
280–287 Owner's or Partners' Capital Accounts
290–297 Owner's or Partners' Withdrawal Accounts
299   Income Summary
For Corporations:
280–285 Capital Stock
286   Paid-in Capital
289   Retained Earnings
290   Treasury Stock
291   Unrealized Gain (Loss) on Marketable Equity Securities
292   Cumulative Foreign Currency Translation Adjustments
299   Income Summary

REVENUE

300 Rooms Revenue
  301 Transient—Regular

302 Transient—Corporate
303 Transient—Package
304 Transient—Preferred Customer
309 Day Use
311 Group—Convention
312 Group—Tour
317 Permanent
318 Meeting Room Rental
319 Other Room Revenue
320 Food Revenue
  321 Food Sales
  322 Banquet Food
  326 Service Charges
  328 Meeting Room Rental
  329 Other Food Revenue
330 Beverage Revenue
  331 Liquor Sales
  332 Wine Sales
  335 Cover Charges
  336 Service Charges
  339 Other Beverage Revenue
340 Telephone Revenue
  341 Local Call Revenue
  342 Long-Distance Call Revenue
  343 Service Charges
  345 Commissions
  346 Pay Station Revenue
  349 Other Telephone Revenue
350 Gift Shop Revenue
360 Garage and Parking Revenue
  361 Parking and Storage
  362 Merchandise Sales
  369 Other Garage and Parking Revenue
370 Space Rentals
  371 Clubs
  372 Offices
  373 Stores
  379 Other Rental Income
380 Other Income
  381 Concessions
  382 Laundry/Valet Commissions
  383 Games and Vending Machines
  384 In-house Movies
  385 Cash Discounts
  386 Interest Income
  387 Foreign Currency Exchange Gains

388 Salvage
389 Other
390 Allowances
    391 Rooms Allowance
    392 Food Allowance
    393 Beverage Allowance
    394 Telephone Allowance
    395 Gift Shop Allowance
    396 Garage and Parking Allowance
    399 Other Allowance

COST OF SALES

420 Cost of Food Sales
    421 Food Purchases
    427 Trade Discounts
    428 Transportation Charges
    429 Other Cost of Food Sales
430 Cost of Beverage Sales
    431 Liquor Purchases
    432 Wine Purchases
    433 Beer Purchases
    434 Other Beverage Purchases
    437 Trade Discounts
    438 Transportation Charges
    439 Other Cost of Beverage Sales
440 Cost of Telephone Calls
    441 Local Calls
    442 Long-Distance Calls
450 Cost of Gift Shop Sales
    451 Gift Shop Purchases
    457 Trade Discounts
    458 Transportation Charges
460 Cost of Garage and Parking Sales
    461 Garage and Parking Purchases
    467 Trade Discounts
    468 Transportation Charges
490 Cost of Employee Meals
492 Bottle Deposit Refunds
495 Grease and Bone Sales Revenue
496 Empty Bottle/Barrel Sales Revenue

PAYROLL

510 Salaries and Wages
    511–519 Departmental Management and Supervisory Staff
    521–539 Departmental Line Employees

550 Payroll Taxes
    551 Payroll Taxes—FICA
    552 Payroll Taxes—FUTA
    553 Payroll Taxes—SUTA
    558 Workers' Compensation
560 Employee Benefits
    561 Vacation, Holiday, and Sick Pay
    564 Medical Insurance
    565 Life Insurance
    566 Dental Insurance
    567 Disability
    568 Pension and Profit Sharing Contributions
    569 Employee Meals
599 Payroll Tax and Benefit Allocation

OTHER EXPENSES

600 Operating Supplies
    601 Cleaning Supplies
    602 Guest Supplies
    603 Paper Supplies
    604 Postage and Telegrams
    605 Printing and Stationery
    606 Menus
    607 Utensils
610 Linen, China, Glassware, etc.
    611 China
    612 Glassware
    613 Silver
    614 Linen
    618 Uniforms
621 Contract Cleaning Expenses
623 Laundry and Dry Cleaning Expenses
624 Laundry Supplies
625 Licenses
627 Kitchen Fuel
628 Music and Entertainment Expenses
629 Reservations Expenses
630 Information Systems Expenses
    631 Hardware Maintenance
    632 Software Maintenance
    635 Service Bureau Fees
    639 Other Information Systems Expenses
640 Human Resources Expenses
    641 Dues and Subscriptions
    642 Employee Housing
    643 Employee Relations

644 Medical Expenses
645 Recruitment
646 Relocation
647 Training
648 Transportation
650 Administrative Expenses
   651 Credit Card Commissions
   652 Donations
   653 Insurance—General
   654 Credit and Collections Expenses
   655 Professional Fees
   656 Losses and Damages
   657 Provision for Doubtful Accounts
   658 Cash Over/Short
   659 Travel and Entertainment
660 Marketing Expenses
   661 Commissions
   662 Direct Mail Expenses
   663 In-house Graphics
   664 Outdoor Advertising
   665 Point-of-Sale Materials
   666 Print Materials
   667 Radio and Television Expenses
   668 Selling Aids
   669 Franchise Fees
670 Property Operation Expenses
   671 Building Supplies
   672 Electrical and Mechanical Equipment
   673 Elevators
   674 Engineering Supplies
   675 Furniture, Fixtures, Equipment, and Decor
   676 Grounds and Landscaping
   677 Painting and Decorating
   678 Removal of Waste Matter
   679 Swimming Pool Expenses
680 Utility Costs
   681 Electrical Cost
   682 Fuel Cost
   686 Steam Cost
   687 Water Cost
   689 Other Utility Costs
690 Guest Transportation
   691 Fuel and Oil
   693 Insurance
   695 Repairs and Maintenance
   699 Other Expenses

FIXED CHARGES

700 Management Fees
710 Rent or Lease Expenses
    711 Land
    712 Buildings
    713 Equipment
    714 Telecommunications Equipment
    715 Information Systems Equipment
    716 Software (includes any license fees)
    717 Vehicles
720 Tax Expense
    721 Real Estate Taxes
    722 Personal Property Taxes
    723 Utility Taxes
    724 Business and Occupation Taxes
730 Building and Content Insurance
740 Interest Expense
    741 Mortgage Interest
    742 Notes Payable Interest
    743 Interest on Capital Leases
    744 Amortization of Deferred Financing Costs
750 Depreciation and Amortization
    751 Building and Improvements
    752 Leaseholds and Leasehold Improvements
    753 Furniture and Fixtures
    754 Machinery and Equipment
    755 Information Systems Equipment
    756 Automobiles and Trucks
    757 Capital Leases
    758 Preopening Expenses
770 Gain or Loss on Sale of Property
790 Income Taxes
    791 Current Federal Income Tax
    792 Deferred Federal Income Tax
    795 Current State Income Tax
    796 Deferred State Income Tax

Section 15
Simplified Bookkeeping for
Limited Service Properties

Since all businesses must keep records of cash received and cash paid out, the simplest bookkeeping system is to keep records on a cash basis. The forms that follow, Cash Receipts Journal and Cash Disbursements Journal, may serve to simplify the bookkeeping procedures for limited-service lodging properties while still providing owners and/or operators with the information to properly prepare financial statements.

All cash receipts should be entered in the Cash Receipts Journal. The cash received from each guest should be listed in the appropriate column for the type of merchandise sold or service rendered. At the end of the month, amounts recorded in the columns should be totaled. The total for column 1, Cash Received, should equal the sum of the total dollar amounts of columns 2 through 8. Once the Cash Receipts Journal is in balance, column totals for Rooms, Food, Telecommunications, Garage and Parking, and Sales Tax should be posted to the proper accounts in the General Ledger. The individual items listed in the Other Income and the General columns should be posted to the appropriate General Ledger accounts listed in columns 7 and 8.

Once cash receipts are entered in the Cash Receipts Journal, they should be deposited in the bank intact. Cash receipts should not be used to make cash disbursements. Cash disbursements should be made by check. When this is not practical, cash disbursements should be paid out from a petty cash fund. The petty cash fund should be kept on an imprest basis--that is, it should be set at a fixed amount and replenished from time to time with funds from the general bank account.

All cash disbursements should be entered in the Cash Disbursements Journal. The check number should be entered in column 1 and the amount of the check should be entered in column 2. The amount should then be distributed to appropriate account classifications in columns 3 through 9. When amounts are charged to Rooms; Cost of Items Purchased for Resale; Property Operation, Maintenance, and Utility Costs; General; or Other, the name of the appropriate account classification should be listed along with the proper amount. For example, cash disbursements for swimming pool expenses should be listed under Other.

A record of petty cash disbursements should be kept following the same form as the Cash Disbursements Journal. When a check is drawn from the general bank account to replenish the petty cash fund, accounts and amounts on the petty cash disbursements sheet should be transferred to the Cash Disbursements Journal.

At the end of the month, amounts recorded in the columns of the Cash Disbursements Journal should be totaled. The total of column 2 should equal the sum of the total dollar amounts of columns 3 through 9. The totals of columns 2, 3, and 4

199

should be posted to the proper accounts in the General Ledger. The individual items entered in columns 5, 6, 7, 8, and 9 should be posted to the appropriate General Ledger accounts.

The Cash Receipts Journal and the Cash Disbursements Journal will provide a complete record of all cash transactions of the small lodging property. Also, the General Ledger accounts will reflect the financial and operating condition of the property on a cash basis. However, these records will not reflect amounts that are due to the property, nor will they reflect amounts that have not yet been paid for supplies or services. When these amounts are minor, some properties may consider it to be impractical to do the necessary bookkeeping to record them. However, in many cases, a complete financial picture is desired and it is essential that the receivables and payables be entered in the records. This accrual basis of record keeping is explained in the following paragraphs.

The accrual basis of record keeping transforms the Cash Receipts Journal into a Sales and Cash Receipts Journal by adding two columns, both labeled Accounts Receivable. Accounts Receivable, column 2, represents a second method of payment column. An entry is made in column 1 (Cash Received) or column 2 (Accounts Receivable) based on whether the sale is a cash or credit transaction. Accounts Receivable, column 10, is used to record a payment received on an account receivable. The remaining columns are completed in a manner similar to cash bookkeeping procedures.

At the end of the month, the dollar amounts in the columns are totaled. The sum of the totals of columns 1 and 2 should equal the sum of the totals of columns 3 through 10. If the Sales and Cash Receipts Journal is in balance, the amounts can be posted to the General Ledger. The total of column 2, Accounts Receivable, is posted as a debit to the ledger account, while the total from column 10 is posted as a credit to the account.

The accrual basis of record keeping makes similar format changes to the Cash Disbursements Journal by adding two columns, both labeled Accounts Payable. Accounts Payable, column 3, is used to record purchases made on account. If cash is paid at the time of purchase, entries are made in columns 1 and 2. Accounts Payable, column 11, is used to record payments made on account. The remaining columns are completed in a manner similar to cash bookkeeping procedures.

At the end of the month, the dollar amounts in the various columns are totaled. The sum of the totals of columns 2 and 3 should equal the sum of the totals of columns 4 through 11. If the Purchases and Cash Disbursements Journal is in balance, the amounts can be posted to the General Ledger. The total of column 3, Accounts Payable, is posted as a credit to the ledger account, while the total from column 11 is posted as a debit to the account. All of the remaining columns are posted in a manner similar to the cash bookkeeping procedures discussed previously.

CASH RECEIPTS JOURNAL (Cash Basis)

Month of _____

Date	Room No.	Name	1 Cash Received (debit)	2 Rooms (credit)	3 Food (credit)	4 Telecommu-nications (credit)	5 Garage/Parking (credit)	6 Sales Tax (credit)	7 Other Income Account | Amount (credit)		8 General Account | Amount (credit)	

CASH DISBURSEMENTS JOURNAL (Cash Basis)

Month of _____

Date	1 Check No.	2 Amounts Paid (credit)	3 Salaries and Wages (debit)	4 Employee Benefits (debit)	5 Rooms Account | Amount (debit)		6 Cost of Items Purchased for Resale Account | Amount (debit)	7 Property Operation Maintenance, and Utility Costs Account | Amount (debit)	8 General Account | Amount (debit)		9 Other Account | Amount (debit)	

SALES AND CASH RECEIPTS JOURNAL (Accrual Basis)

Month of _____

Date	Room No.	Name	1 Cash Received (debit)	2 Accounts Receivable (debit)	3 Rooms (credit)	4 Food (credit)	5 Telecommu- nications (credit)	6 Garage/ Parking (credit)	7 Sales Tax (credit)	8 Other Income Account | Amount (credit)	9 General Account | Amount (credit)	10 Accounts Receivable (credit)

PURCHASES AND CASH DISBURSEMENTS JOURNAL (Accrual Basis)

Month of _____

Date	1 Check No.	2 Amounts Paid (credit)	3 Accounts Payable (credit)	4 Salaries and Wages (debit)	5 Employee Benefits (debit)	6 Rooms Account | Amount (debit)	7 Cost of Items Purchased for Resale Account | Amount (debit)	8 Property Operation Maintenance, and Utility Costs Account | Amount (debit)	9 General Account | Amount (debit)	10 Other Account | Amount (debit)	11 Accounts Payable (debit)

Part IV
Expense Dictionary

Expense Dictionary

INTRODUCTION

This dictionary is designed to help members of the lodging industry classify, in accordance with the *Uniform System of Accounts for the Lodging Industry*, the numerous expense and payroll-related items encountered in their daily work. It will also serve as a ready reference for the executive, the manager, and the purchasing agent, showing them to which account or expense group the accounting department will charge each expense item.

It should be noted, however, that not all property expenditures are recorded as expenses. An expenditure made to purchase an item with a useful life of more than one year typically will be capitalized. That is, the amount will be included as an asset on the balance sheet and expensed through depreciation or amortization over the item's useful life. There are some exceptions to this general rule.

The materiality of the expenditure may influence whether the expenditure is capitalized or expensed. Consider, for example, a minor expenditure such as the purchase of an inexpensive desk calculator for $50. Because this item has a useful life of more than one year, it should be capitalized. However, in this case, the benefit of capitalizing the item may not outweigh the cost of setting up and maintaining the depreciation records. Consequently, the expenditure may be expensed. The dollar amount that determines whether expenditures are capitalized or expensed is a matter of judgment. Once the amount is established, it should become part of company or property policy and be followed consistently.

There are other expenditures that extend the life of an asset or add value to an asset. Generally accepted accounting principles require that these types of expenditures be capitalized and depreciated over the estimated remaining useful life of the asset. The most common example is an expenditure to repair property and equipment. If the repair expenditure only restores the value of the asset to its condition prior to the repair, the expenditure should be expensed. However, if the expenditure extends the life of the asset or increases the value of the asset, the expenditure should be capitalized.

Finally, there are expenditures which are normally expensed, but which, under certain circumstances, are more properly capitalized. Examples include interest costs incurred during the development, construction, or renovation of a property and software development costs associated with the purchase of a new computer system. While interest costs and software costs may be expensed in some situations, generally accepted accounting principles prescribe that, when these expenditures are incurred as part of the acquisition of the asset, it is proper to include these expenditures in the total amount that is capitalized. Each property's controller should be familiar with the guidelines established by the appropriate accounting principle for the treatment of these and other similar expenditures.

How to Read the Expense Dictionary

GUIDE TO ABBREVIATIONS	
Abbreviation	**Department/Function/Item**
A&G	Administrative and General
Adv.	Advertising and Merchandising
China	China, Glassware, Silver, and Linen
Depr. & Amort.	Depreciation and Amortization
Elec. & Mech.	Electrical and Mechanical Equipment
HR	Human Resources
Mktg.	Marketing
POM	Property Operation and Maintenance
Prtg. & Stat.	Printing and Stationery
PTEB	Payroll Taxes and Employee Benefits
RPTI	Rent, Property Taxes, and Insurance

The Expense Dictionary is divided into two columns. Column I lists expense items alphabetically. Column II identifies the accounts to which the expense items would be charged. Items purchased for direct sale in any department are not included, since their distribution is obviously direct to the cost of sales of the department concerned.

Column II lists expense accounts in a number of ways. The following is a short explanation of the various forms these listings can take.

If a single word or phrase is listed, it is the departmental schedule that the item would be charged to. For example, the entry for **Fuel** is **Utility Costs.** The Utility Costs schedule would then ask you to list various fuels separately.

If a department, operational function, or cost center is followed by a dash, the entry following the dash is the account charged within that department, operational function, or cost center. For example, the entry for **Bedspreads** is **Rooms—Linen.**

Some expenses are broken down even further. For example, the entry for **Outdoor Advertising** is **Mktg.—Adv.—Outdoor.** Marketing is the department, Advertising and Merchandising is the function within the department, and Outdoor is the account. Sometimes the last element in such a breakdown refers to an account that is not listed on the schedule as presented earlier in this book but is addressed in the discussion of that schedule. For example, the entry for **Hangers** is **Rooms—Operating Supplies—Guest Supplies.**

If more than one department or cost center can charge a particular expense item to accounts with the same name, the departments or cost centers are separated by diagonal slashes. For example, the entry for **Professional Entertainers** is **Food/Beverage—Music & Entertainment.**

If the same item is charged by different departments or cost centers to different accounts, departments and accounts are listed consecutively and separated by semicolons. For example, the entry for **Drinking Glasses** is **Rooms—Operating Supplies—Guest Supplies; Food/Beverage—China.**

When one account is followed by another entire account in parentheses, the first is more specific than the second. If your property does not use the more specific breakdown, use the more general account listed in the parentheses. For example, the entry for **Employee Lodging** is **HR—Employee Housing (A&G—HR).**

Sometimes, one department, operational function, or cost center can charge a particular expense item to more than one account. In this case, the accounts following the dash are separated by slashes. For example, the entry for **Beeper Rental** is **A&G—Comm. Systems/Operating Supplies and Equip.**

Expense Dictionary

Item	Classification

A

Accountants' Fees	A&G—Professional Fees
Acids	Rooms—Operating Supplies—Cleaning Supplies; House Laundry—Cleaning Supplies
Adding Machine Tapes	All Departments—Operating Supplies
Advertising Agency Fees	Mktg.—Fees & Commissions—Agency Fees
Advertising—Direct Mail	Mktg.—Adv.—Direct Mail
Advertising—Directories	Mktg.—Adv.—Media
Advertising—Outdoor	Mktg.—Adv.—Outdoor
Advertising—Publications	Mktg.—Adv.—Media
Advertising—Radio & TV	Mktg.—Adv.—Media
Air-Cooling Systems Repairs	POM—HVAC
Airport Transportation—Not Chargeable to Guest	Trans—Contract Services (A&G—Travel)
Alarm Service—Fire or Burglar	Security—Contract Services (A&G—Security)
Amortization—Leasehold Improvements	Depr. & Amort.—Leaseholds & Leasehold Improvements
Amortization—Mortgage Expense	Interest Expense
Answering Machines	All Departments—Telecommunications
Armored Car Service	Security—Armored Car Service (A&G—Security)
Ash Trays	Rooms/Food/Beverage—China
Association Dues—Mktg. Employees	Mktg.—Selling—Dues & Subscriptions
Association Dues—Other than Mktg. Employees	A&G—Dues & Subscriptions
Athletic Equipment for Employees	HR—Employee Relations (A&G—HR)
Attorney's Fees—For Collections	A&G—Credit and Collection
Attorney's Fees—Other Than Collections	A&G—Professional Fees
Audit Fees—Public Accountants	A&G—Professional Fees
Auto Rental	Trans.—Contract Services (A&G—Travel)
Auto Supplies—Used by Property	POM—Vehicle Maintenance

Item	Classification
Auto/Truck Repair—Property Use	Trans.—Repairs & Maint. (POM—Vehicle Maintenance)
Awards—Employees	HR—Employee Relations (A&G—HR; PTEB—Employee Benefits—Other)
Awnings—Cleaning	Rooms/Food/Beverage—Laundry & Dry Cleaning

B

Item	Classification
Bad Debts	A&G—Provision for Doubtful Accounts (see also Balance Sheet—Allowance for Doubtful Accounts)
Baggage Checking Supplies	Rooms—Operating Supplies—Prtg. & Stat.
Bags (Laundry)	House Laundry—Laundry Supplies
Bags (Retail Outlet)	All Departments—Operating Supplies
Bank Checks, Charges	A&G—Bank Charges
Bank Exchange on Checks & Currency ...	A&G—Bank Charges
Banquet Reports	Food/Beverage—Operating Supplies—Prtg. & Stat.
Bar Appetizers	Beverage—Gratis Food
Bar Utensils	Beverage—Operating Supplies—Other
Basket Liners, Waste Paper	Rooms/Food/Beverage—Operating Supplies—Guest Supplies
Bath Mats	Rooms—Linen
Bathing Caps	Rooms—Operating Supplies—Guest Supplies
Batteries	All Departments—Operating Supplies
Bedspreads	Rooms—Linen
Bedspreads—Cleaning	Rooms—Laundry & Dry Cleaning
Beeper Rental	A&G—Comm. Systems/Operating Supplies & Equip.
Beverage Licenses	Beverage—Licenses
Beverage Lists	Food/Beverage—Operating Supplies—Prtg. & Stat.
Beverage Mixers	Beverage—Cost of Beverage
Beverage Spoons	Beverage—Operating Supplies—Other
Beverage Stirrers—Glass	Beverage—Operating Supplies—Other
Bicycles—Repair/Rental	Other Operated Departments—Contract Services/Operating Supplies
Billboards	Mktg.—Adv.—Outdoor
Billing Statements/Invoices	A&G—Prtg. & Stat.
Binders	A&G—Operating Supplies & Equip.; Rooms—Operating Supplies—Prtg. & Stat.
Binding System Accessories	A&G—Operating Supplies & Equip.
Blankets	Rooms—Linen
Blankets—Cleaning	Rooms—Laundry & Dry Cleaning
Boiler Inspection	POM—Elec. & Mech.

Item	Classification
Boiler Repairs	POM—Elec. & Mech.
Book Matches (Guest)	Rooms/Food/Beverage/Other Operated Departments—Operating Supplies—Guest Supplies
Books	Rooms—Operating Supplies—Prtg. & Stat.
Books for Guest Library	Rooms—Operating Supplies—Guest Supplies
Books—Technical	All Departments—Training (A&G—Dues & Subscriptions)
Booths—Trade Shows	Mktg.—Selling—Trade Shows
Bottle Openers (Loose)	Rooms/Food/Beverage—Operating Supplies—Guest Supplies
Boutonnieres	Food/Beverage—Operating Supplies—Guest Supplies
Bowls	Food/Beverage—China
Bread and Butter Plates	Food—China
Brochures	Mktg.—Adv.—In-House Graphics
Brooms	Rooms/Food/Beverage—Operating Supplies—Cleaning Supplies
Brushes—Cleaning	Rooms/Food/Beverage—Operating Supplies—Cleaning Supplies
Brushes—Hair	Rooms—Operating Supplies—Guest Supplies
Building & Contents Insurance	RPTI—Insurance—Building & Contents
Building Repairs	POM—Building Supplies
Bulletin Board Supplies	Rooms—Operating Supplies
Burglar Alarm Service	Security—Contract Services (A&G—Security)
Business Cards	A&G—Prtg. & Stat.
Buttons	Rooms—Operating Supplies—Guest Supplies

C

Item	Classification
Cable TV	Rooms—Cable/Satellite Television
Calculators	A&G—Operating Supplies & Equip.
Calendars and Diaries	A&G—Operating Supplies & Equip.
Candles	Rooms—Operating Supplies
Candy	Rooms/Food/Beverage—Operating Supplies—Guest Supplies
Carafes	Rooms—Operating Supplies—Guest Supplies; Food/Beverage—China
Cardboard Boxes	Food/Beverage—Operating Supplies—Paper Supplies
Carfares, Taxis	A&G—Travel
Carpet Repairs	POM—Floor Covering
Carpet Sweepers	Rooms/Food/Beverage—Operating Supplies—Cleaning Supplies
Cash Boxes	A&G—Operating Supplies & Equip.

Item	Classification
Cash Overage & Shortage	A&G—Cash Overages & Shortages
Cash Register—Repairs	POM—Elec. & Mech.
Cashier Envelopes	A&G—Operating Supplies & Equip.
Cashier Forms	A&G—Operating Supplies & Equip.
Charge Vouchers	Rooms/Food/Beverage—Operating Supplies—Prtg. & Stat.
Checks—Bank	A&G—Bank Charges
Check Writer Machines	A&G—Operating Supplies & Equip.
Checking Supplies	Food/Beverage—Operating Supplies—Paper Supplies
Chemicals—Fire Extinguisher	POM—Life/Safety
Chemicals—Laundry	House Laundry—Laundry Supplies
China—F&B Use	Food/Beverage—China
Christmas Gifts—Employees	HR—Employee Relations (A&G—HR; PTEB—Employee Benefits—Other)
Christmas Trees and Decorations	Rooms/Food/Beverage—Other
Cleaning Compounds	Rooms/Food/Beverage—Operating Supplies—Cleaning Supplies
Cleaning Supplies	Rooms/Food/Beverage/etc.—Operating Supplies—Cleaning Supplies
Cleaning Supplies—Food	Food/Beverage—Operating Supplies—Cleaning Supplies
Clinic Employees	HR—Medical Expenses (A&G—HR)
Clipboards	A&G—Operating Supplies & Equip.
Clips	Rooms—Operating Supplies—Prtg. & Stat.
Cocktail Napkins—Paper	Food/Beverage—Operating Supplies—Paper Supplies
Coffee Bags	Food/Beverage—Operating Supplies
Coffee (Free)	Rooms—Operating Supplies—Guest Supplies
Coffee Pots	Food/Beverage—China
Coffee Urn Repairs	POM—Elec. & Mech.
Coin/Currency Bag Seals	A&G—Operating Supplies & Equip.
Coin/Currency Equipment	A&G—Operating Supplies & Equip.
Coin Handling Equipment	A&G—Operating Supplies & Equip.
Coin Wrappers	A&G—Operating Supplies & Equip.
Collection Fees	A&G—Credit and Collection
Combs (Guest)	Rooms—Operating Supplies—Guest Supplies
Commissions—Beverage	Beverage—Salaries & Wages
Commissions—Credit Card Charge	A&G—Credit Card Commissions
Commissions—F&B (Employees)	Food/Beverage—Salaries & Wages
Commissions—Tour Agencies	Rooms—Commissions
Complimentary Beverage	Mktg.—Selling—Complimentary Guests; Rooms—Complimentary Guest Services

Item	Classification
Complimentary Food	Mktg.—Selling—Complimentary Guests; Rooms—Complimentary Guest Services
Complimentary Parking	Mktg.—Selling—Complimentary Guests
Complimentary Rooms—Musicians & Entertainers	Food/Beverage—Music & Entertainment
Compotes	Food/Beverage—China
Computer Books	All Departments—Operating Supplies
Computer Forms—Commercial	All Departments—Operating Supplies—Paper Supplies
Computer Forms—Printed	A&G—Prtg. & Stat.
Computer Manuals—Commercial	Information Systems—Training (A&G—Information Systems)
Computer Manuals—Printed	Information Systems—Prtg. & Stat. (A&G—Information Systems)
Computer Printer Paper	All Departments—Operating Supplies
Computer Rentals	RPTI—Rent—Information Systems Equip.
Computer Software—Commercial Applications	All Departments—Operating Supplies; Information Systems—Software—Commercial Applications (A&G—Information Systems)
Computer Supplies and Accessories	All Departments—Operating Supplies
Consultant Fees, Professional	All Departments—Contract Services
Containers—Liquid, Paper	Food/Beverage—Operating Supplies
Contract Cleaning	Rooms—Contract Services
Contract Cleaning—Dining Room	Food/Beverage—Contract Services
Contract Cleaning—Fumigation	Rooms/Food/Beverage—Contract Services
Contract Cleaning—Lobbies	Rooms—Contract Services
Contract Cleaning—Windows	Rooms/Food/Beverage—Contract Services
Contract Entertainment	Food/Beverage—Music & Entertainment
Contract Exterminating	Rooms/Food/Beverage—Contract Services
Contributions	A&G—Donations
Controller's Reports	A&G—Operating Supplies & Equip.
Convention Bureau	Mktg.—Selling—Dues & Subscriptions
Cooking Utensils in Kitchenette Apts.	Rooms—Operating Supplies—Guest Supplies
Copier Paper	A&G—Operating Supplies & Equip.
Copier—Rental (lease)	All Departments—Contract Services
Copier Toner	A&G—Operating Supplies & Equip.
Copying Service	A&G—Prtg. & Stat.
Copyright Licenses	Food/Beverage—Licenses
Corkscrews	Food/Beverage—Operating Supplies
Corsages	Rooms/Food/Beverage—Operating Supplies—Guest Supplies
Court Fees	A&G—Professional Fees
CPU Stands	A&G—Operating Supplies & Equip.
Credit Application Forms	A&G—Prtg. & Stat.
Credit Card Commissions	A&G—Credit Card Commissions

Item	Classification
Credit & Collection Expenses	A&G—Credit and Collection
Credit Reports	A&G—Credit and Collection
Cups	Food/Beverage—China
Cups—Bouillon, Coffee, Custard, Tea	Food/Beverage—China
Cups—Paper	Food/Beverage—Operating Supplies— Paper Supplies
Cups—Paper (Employee)	PTEB—Employee Benefits—Meals
Cups—Paper (Guest)	Rooms/Food/Beverage—Operating Supplies—Guest Supplies
Currency Bill Straps	A&G—Operating Supplies & Equip.
Curtain Cleaning	Rooms/Food/Beverage—Laundry & Dry Cleaning
Curtains—Shower	Rooms—Linen

D

Item	Classification
Daily Reports	A&G—Prtg. & Stat.
Damaged Articles—Guest	A&G—Loss & Damage
Data Binders and Accessories	All Departments—Operating Supplies
Data Cartridges and Tapes	Information Systems—Operating Supplies & Equip. (A&G—Information Systems)
Data Processing—Rent	RPTI—Rent—Information Systems Equip.
Data Processing—Supplies	Information Systems—Operating Supplies & Equip. (A&G—Information Systems)
Data Systems and Storage Files	All Departments—Operating Supplies (A&G—Information Systems)
Decorating and Painting	POM—Painting & Decorating
Decorations	Rooms—Operating Supplies—Other
Deodorants	Rooms—Operating Supplies—Guest Supplies
Depreciation—Building	Depr. & Amort.—Buildings
Depreciation—Equipment	Depr. & Amort.—Furnishings & Equip.
Desk Accessories (Employee)	All Departments—Operating Supplies
Desk Pads (Employee)	Rooms/Food/Beverage—Operating Supplies—Prtg. & Stat.; A&G—Operating Supplies
Desk Pads (Guest)	Rooms—Operating Supplies—Guest Supplies
Detective Service	Security—Contract Services (A&G— Security)
Detergents	Food/Beverage—Operating Supplies— Cleaning Supplies
Direct Mail Expenses—Outside Service . . .	Mktg.—Adv.—Direct Mail
Directional Signs (Inside Building)	Mktg.—Adv.—In-House Graphics
Directories	Rooms—Operating Supplies—Prtg. & Stat.

Item	Classification
Directors' Expense	A&G—Head Office
Directory Advertising	Mktg.—Adv.—Media
Directory Holders—Telephone	Rooms—Operating Supplies—Prtg. & Stat.; Telecommunications—Other
Dishes	Food/Beverage—China
Dishwasher Repairs	POM—Elec. & Mech.
Dishwashing Compounds	Food/Beverage—Operating Supplies— Cleaning Supplies
Disinfectants	Rooms/Food/Beverage—Operating Supplies—Cleaning Supplies
Diskettes	All Departments—Operating Supplies
Doilies	Food/Beverage—China/Operating Supplies—Paper Supplies
Donations	A&G—Donations
Doubtful Accounts—Provision for	A&G—Provision for Doubtful Accounts
Drapery Cleaning	Rooms/Food/Beverage—Laundry & Dry Cleaning
Drinking Glasses	Rooms—Operating Supplies—Guest Supplies; Food/Beverage—China
Drugs & Other Medical Supplies— Employees	HR—Medical Supplies (A&G—HR)
Dues—Association	A&G—Dues & Subscriptions; Mktg.— Selling—Dues & Subscriptions
Dust Cloths	Rooms—Operating Supplies—Cleaning Supplies

E

Item	Classification
Educational Activities for Employees	HR—Employee Relations (A&G—HR; PTEB—Employee Benefits—Other)
Educational Books & Pamphlets for Employees	HR—Employee Relations (A&G—HR; PTEB—Employee Benefits—Other)
Electric Bulbs	POM—Light Bulbs
Elevator Repairs	POM—Elec. & Mech.
Employee Clinic	HR—Medical Expenses (A&G—HR; PTEB—Employee Benefits—Other)
Employee Credit Union	HR—Other (A&G—HR)
Employee Housing	HR—Employee Housing (A&G—HR)
Employee Investigations	HR—Recruitment (A&G—HR)
Employee Lodging	HR—Employee Housing (A&G—HR)
Employee Meals	All Departments—Employee Benefits— Meals
Employee Relations Expense	HR—Employee Relations (A&G—HR)
Employee Transportation	HR—Trans. (A&G—Trans.)
Employment Agency Fees	HR—Recruitment (A&G—HR)
Engineering Supplies	POM—Engineering Supplies
Entertainment and Music	Food/Beverage—Music & Entertainment
Envelopes—Guest	Rooms—Operating Supplies—Guest Supplies

Item	Classification
Envelopes—Plain	All Departments—Operating Supplies—Paper Supplies
Exchange on Bank Checks & Currency	A&G—Bank Charges
Executive Office Expenses	A&G—Head Office
Express Delivery Charges	All Departments—Other (A&G—Postage)
Extension Cords	POM—Other

F

Item	Classification
Face Cloths (Guest)	Rooms—Linen
Facial Tissues	Rooms—Operating Supplies—Guest Supplies
Fares—Taxicabs—Employees	HR—Transportation (A&G—Transportation); Mktg.—Selling—Travel
Favors	Food/Beverage—Operating Supplies—Guest Supplies
Fax Machine Supplies & Accessories	A&G—Communications Systems; Telecommunications—Prtg. & Stat.
Federal Retirement Taxes	PTEB—Payroll Taxes—Federal Retirement
Federal Unemployment Taxes	PTEB—Payroll Taxes—Federal Unemployment
Fees, Attorneys'—For Collections	A&G—Credit and Collection
Fees, Attorneys'—Other Than Collections	A&G—Professional Fees
Fees, Audit—Public Accountants	A&G—Professional Fees
Fees, Collection	A&G—Credit and Collection
Fees, Court	A&G—Professional Fees
Fees, Franchise	Franchise Fees
Fees, Legal	A&G—Professional Fees
Fees, Management	Management Fees
Fees, Medical (Service to Employees)	HR—Medical Expenses (A&G—HR)
Fees, Medical (Service to Guest)	A&G—Loss and Damage
Fees, Notary	A&G—Professional Fees
Fees, Protest	A&G—Professional Fees
Fees, Stock Transfer Agents	A&G—Professional Fees
Fees, Transfer	A&G—Professional Fees
Fees, Trustees (Handling bonds, etc.)	A&G—Professional Fees
Fertilizer	POM—Grounds & Landscaping
Film Purchase and Developing	A&G—Other
Films	Food/Beverage—Music & Entertainment
Filter paper	Food/Beverage—Operating Supplies—Paper Supplies
Fines	A&G—Other
Fire Alarm Service	Security—Contract Services (A&G—Security)
Fire Axes	POM—Life/Safety
Fire Bucket Sand	POM—Life/Safety
Fire Extinguisher Chemicals	POM—Life/Safety
Firewood for Lobby	Rooms—Operating Supplies

Item	Classification
First Aid Supplies	HR—Medical Expenses (A&G—HR)
Flatware	Food/Beverage—China
Floor plans	Rooms—Operating Supplies—Prtg. & Stat.
Floor wax	Rooms—Operating Supplies—Cleaning Supplies
Floppy Disks	All Departments—Operating Supplies
Flowers	Rooms—Operating Supplies—Guest Supplies
Foil Wrapping	Food/Beverage—Operating Supplies—Paper Supplies
Food—Gratis (Not Used in the Preparation of Mixed Drinks)	Beverage—Gratis Food; Mktg.—Selling—Complimentary Guests
Food Licenses	Food/Beverage—Licenses
Forks	Food/Beverage—China
Forms—General	All Departments—Operating Supplies
Forms—Printed	All Departments—Operating Supplies
Franchise Fees	Franchise Fees
Freight Charges	A&G—Postage; Mktg.—Trade Show
Front Desk Signs	Rooms—Other
Fruit (Guest)	Rooms—Operating Supplies—Guest Supplies; Mktg.—Selling—Complimentary Guests
Fuel	Utility Costs
Fuel—Gas	Utility Costs—Gas
Fuel—Kitchen	Food—Operating Supplies—Other
Fumigators	Rooms/Food/Beverage—Contract Services
Furniture Polish	Rooms/Food/Beverage—Operating Supplies—Cleaning Supplies
Furniture Rental (Public Rooms)	Rooms—Other
Furniture Repairs	POM—Furniture

G

Item	Classification
Garbage Removal	POM—Removal of Waste Matter
Garment Bags	Rooms—Operating Supplies—Guest Supplies
Gas—Cooking	Food—Operating Supplies—Other
Gas—Fuel	Utility Costs—Gas
Gasoline—Motor Vehicles (Company and Employee Use)	POM—Vehicle Maintenance
Gasoline—Motor Vehicles (Guest Transportation)	Trans.—Fuel & Oil (Rooms—Guest Trans.)
Glass Bowls	Food/Beverage—China
Glass Dishes	Food/Beverage—China
Glass Pitchers	Rooms—Operating Supplies—Guest Supplies; Food/Beverage—China

Item	Classification
Glasses—Drinking	Rooms—Operating Supplies—Guest Supplies; Food/Beverage—China
Glasses—Water	Rooms—Operating Supplies—Guest Supplies; Food/Beverage—China
Glassware	Rooms—Operating Supplies—Guest Supplies; Food/Beverage—China
Glue—Office	A&G—Operating Supplies & Equip.
Goblets	Food/Beverage—China
Gratis Food (Not Used in the Preparation of Mixed Drinks)	Beverage—Gratis Food; Mktg—Selling—Complimentary Guests
Gratuities & Christmas Presents (Other Than Employees or Guests)	PTEB—Employee Benefits—Other
Grounds Expense	POM—Grounds & Landscaping
Guest Folios	Rooms—Operating Supplies—Prtg. & Stat.
Guest Soap	Rooms—Operating Supplies—Guest Supplies
Guest Stationery	Rooms—Operating Supplies—Guest Supplies

H

Item	Classification
Hair Nets	Rooms—Operating Supplies—Guest Supplies
Hangers	Rooms—Operating Supplies—Guest Supplies
Help Wanted Ads	HR—Recruitment (A&G—HR)
Holders	Rooms—Operating Supplies—Paper Supplies
Hotel Association Dues	A&G—Dues & Subscriptions
Hotel Sales & Marketing Association Dues	Mktg.—Selling—Dues & Subscriptions
House Publication (for Employees)	HR—Employee Relations (A&G—HR)
Housekeeper and Attendants' Reports	Rooms—Operating Supplies—Prtg. & Stat.
Housing—Employees	HR—Employee Housing (A&G—HR)

I

Item	Classification
Ice/Ice Buckets	Rooms/Food/Beverage—Operating Supplies—Guest Supplies
Insecticides	Rooms/Food/Beverage—Operating Supplies—Cleaning Supplies; POM—Other
Insurance—Building and Contents	RPTI—Insurance—Building & Contents
Insurance—Fire	RPTI—Insurance—Building & Contents
Insurance—General	RPTI—Insurance
Insurance—Group (Nonunion)	PTEB—Employee Benefits—Nonunion Insurance
Insurance—Group (Union)	PTEB—Employee Benefits—Union Insurance
Insurance—Hospitalization (Nonunion Employees)	PTEB—Employee Benefits—Nonunion Insurance

Item	Classification
Insurance—Hospitalization (Union Employees)	PTEB—Employee Benefits—Union Insurance
Insurance—Liability	RPTI—Insurance—Liability
Insurance—Life—Nonunion Employee (Employee Beneficiary)	PTEB—Employee Benefits—Nonunion Insurance
Insurance—Life—Union Employee (Employee Beneficiary)	PTEB—Employee Benefits—Union Insurance
Insurance—Workers' Compensation	PTEB—Employee Benefits—Workers' Compensation Insurance
Interest	Interest Expense
Internal Audit Expense	A&G—Internal Audit
Internal Audit Fees (Chain Properties)	A&G—Internal Audit
Internet—WWW Connection	A&G—Contract Services
Internet Telephone Charges	Mktg.—Selling—Telecommunications; Rooms—Reservations
Interview Expense	HR—Recruitment (A&G—HR)
Investigation of Employees	HR—Recruitment (A&G—HR)

K

Item	Classification
Keyboard Drawers	A&G—Operating Supplies & Equip.
Kitchenette Expenses	Rooms—Operating Supplies—Guest Supplies
Knives	Food/Beverage—China

L

Item	Classification
Ladles	Food/Beverage—China
Landscaping	POM—Grounds & Landscaping
Laser Printer Paper	A&G—Operating Supplies & Equip.
Laser Printer Supplies & Accessories	A&G—Operating Supplies & Equip.
Laundry	Rooms/Food/Beverage/Health Center/ Swimming Pool—Laundry & Dry Cleaning
Leasehold Improvements Amortization	Depr. & Amort.—Leaseholds & Leasehold Improvements
Legal Expenses	A&G—Professional Fees
Legal Fees	A&G—Professional Fees
Letters for Bulletin/Sign Boards	A&G—Operating Supplies & Equip.
Licenses—Beverages, Federal	Beverage—Licenses
Licenses—Beverages, Municipal	Beverage—Licenses
Licenses—Beverages, State	Beverage—Licenses
Licenses—Canopy	A&G—Other
Licenses—Checkrooms	A&G—Other
Licenses—Dance	Food/Beverage—Licenses
Licenses—Elevator	POM—Elevators
Licenses—Engineering	POM—Other
Licenses—General	A&G—Other
Licenses—Gift Shop	Other Operated Departments—Other
Licenses—Guestroom	Rooms—Operating Supplies—Other

Item	Classification
Licenses—Ice Cream	Food—Licenses
Licenses—Laundry	House Laundry—Other
Licenses—Locksmith	POM—Other
Licenses—Mercantile	Food/Beverage—Licenses
Licenses—Music	Food/Beverage—Licenses
Licenses—Public Rooms	Rooms—Operating Supplies—Other
Licenses and Permits	A&G—Other
Limousine	Trans.—Other (A&G—Trans.); Rooms—Guest Trans.
Linen	Rooms—Linen
Linen Napkins	Food/Beverage—China
Linen Rental	Rooms—Linen; Food/Beverage—China
Linen Sheets	Rooms—Linen
Linen Towels	Rooms—Linen; Food/Beverage—China
Liners	Rooms/Food/Beverage—Operating Supplies—Paper Supplies
Literature—Educational for Employees	HR—Employee Relations (A&G—HR; PTEB—Employee Benefits—Other)
Liquid Containers, Paper	Food/Beverage—Operating Supplies—Paper Supplies
Lobby Cleaning (on Contract)	Rooms—Contract Services
Lobby Signs	Mktg.—Adv.—In-House Graphics
Lock Repairs	POM—Elec. & Mech.
Lodging of Employees	HR—Employee Housing (A&G—HR)
Log Books	Rooms/Food/Beverage—Operating Supplies—Prtg. & Stat.; A&G—Operating Supplies & Equip.
Lost & Damaged Articles (Guest)	A&G—Loss & Damage
Lost & Found Reports	A&G—Other

M

Item	Classification
Machine Stands	A&G—Operating Supplies & Equip.
Magazine Advertising	Mktg.—Adv.—Media
Magazines (Guest)	Rooms—Operating Supplies—Guest Supplies
Magazines—Trade	A&G—Dues & Subscriptions; Mktg.—Selling—Dues & Subscriptions
Mail Bags	A&G—Operating Supplies & Equip./Postage
Mail Chute Rentals	A&G—Operating Supplies & Equip./Postage
Mailing Lists	Mktg.—Adv.—Direct Mail
Maintenance—Electric Submeters	POM—Contract Services
Maintenance Contracts—Electric Signs	POM—Contract Services
Maintenance Contracts—Office Equipment	A&G—Contract Services
Management Fees	Management Fees
Manuals—Service (Instructional Materials)	All Departments—Training
Marketing Service Fees	Mktg.—Fees & Commissions—Other

Item	Classification
Marquee Licenses	A&G—Other
Matches	Rooms—Operating Supplies—Guest Supplies
Mats—Bath	Rooms—Linen
Mats—Floor	POM—Floor Covering
Mats—Rubber	POM—Floor Covering
Mattress Protectors	Rooms—Linen
Meals—Employees	All Departments—Employee Benefits
Meals and Entertainment—Outside	A&G/Mktg.—Meals & Entertainment
Mechanical Music	Food/Beverage—Music & Entertainment
Medical Fees (Service to Employees)	HR—Medical Expenses (A&G—HR)
Medical Supplies (for Employees)	HR—Medical Expenses (A&G—HR)
Membership Dues—Associations	A&G—Dues & Subscriptions
Membership Dues—Marketing Employees	Mktg.—Selling—Dues & Subscriptions
Menus	Food/Beverage—Operating Supplies—Menus
Mercantile Agency Subscriptions	A&G—Dues & Subscriptions
Message Envelopes (Telephone)	Telecommunications—Prtg. & Stat.
Metal Polish	Rooms/Food/Beverage—Operating Supplies—Cleaning Supplies
Microfiche Supplies	A&G—Operating Supplies & Equip.
Mixing Bowls	Food—Operating Supplies—Utensils
Mixing Spoons	Food—Operating Supplies—Utensils
Mop Handles and Wringers	Rooms/Food/Beverage—Operating Supplies—Cleaning Supplies
Mops	Rooms/Food/Beverage—Operating Supplies—Cleaning Supplies
Mortgage Interest on First Mortgage	Interest Expense
Motor Repairs	POM—Elec. & Mech.
Mouse	All Departments—Operating Supplies
Mouse Traps	Rooms—Operating Supplies—Cleaning Supplies
Mouthwash	Rooms—Operating Supplies—Guest Supplies
Municipal Licenses—Beverages	Beverage—Licenses
Municipal Taxes—Beverages	Beverage—Licenses
Music and Entertainment	Food/Beverage—Music & Entertainment
Music Licenses	Food/Beverage—Music & Entertainment
Musicians	Food/Beverage—Music & Entertainment

N

Item	Classification
Name Badges	All Departments—Operating Supplies
Napkins—Linen	Food/Beverage—China
Napkins—Paper	Food/Beverage—Operating Supplies—Paper Supplies
Needle and Thread	Rooms/Food/Beverage—Operating Supplies—Guest Supplies

Item	Classification
Newspapers	Rooms—Operating Supplies—Guest Supplies
Notary Fees	A&G—Professional Fees
Notary Fees—Collection of Accounts	A&G—Credit and Collection

O

Item	Classification
Office Supplies and Accessories	A&G—Operating Supplies & Equip.
Outdoor Advertising	Mktg.—Adv.—Outdoor
Overages & Shortages—Cash	A&G—Cash Overages & Shortages

P

Item	Classification
Pager Rental	A&G—Internal Communications
Pails	Rooms/Food/Beverage—Operating Supplies—Cleaning Supplies
Paint Cleaners	Rooms—Operating Supplies—Cleaning Supplies; POM—Painting & Decorating
Pamphlets—Educational or Instructional (for Employees)	HR—Employee Relations (A&G—HR)
Paper Bags	Food/Beverage—Operating Supplies—Paper Supplies
Paper Clips	Rooms/Food/Beverage—Operating Supplies—Prtg. & Stat.; A&G—Operating Supplies & Equip.
Paper Cups (Employee)	PTEB—Employee Benefits—Meals
Paper Liners	Rooms/Food/Beverage—Operating Supplies—Paper Supplies; A&G—Operating Supplies & Equip.
Paper Napkins	Rooms/Food/Beverage—Operating Supplies—Paper Supplies
Paper Pads (Employee)	Rooms/Food/Beverage—Operating Supplies—Paper Supplies
Paper Towels (Employee)	Rooms/Food/Beverage/etc.—Operating Supplies—Paper Supplies
Parchment	Food/Beverage—Operating Supplies—Paper Supplies
Paste	Rooms/Food/Beverage—Operating Supplies—Prtg. & Stat.; A&G—Operating Supplies & Equip.
Pastry Bags	Food—Operating Supplies—Paper Supplies
Payroll and Tax Forms	A&G—Operating Supplies
Pencil Sharpeners	Rooms/Food/Beverage/etc.—Operating Supplies—Prtg. & Stat.; A&G—Operating Supplies & Equip.
Pens and Pencils (Employees)	Rooms/Food/Beverage/etc.—Operating Supplies—Prtg. & Stat.; A&G—Operating Supplies & Equip.

Item	Classification
Pens and Pencils (Guests)	Rooms/Food/Beverage—Operating Supplies—Guest Supplies
Pensions (Nonunion)	PTEB—Nonunion Pension
Pensions (Union)	PTEB—Union Pension
Personnel Forms—General	HR—Prtg. & Stat. (A&G—HR)
Personnel Forms—Printed	HR—Prtg. & Stat. (A&G—HR)
Pest Control	Rooms/Food/Beverage/POM—Other
Petty Cash Forms	A&G—Operating Supplies & Equip.
Physicians' Fees (Employees)	HR—Medical Expenses (A&G—HR)
Piano Rental	Food/Beverage—Music & Entertainment
Pins (Employee)	A&G—Operating Supplies & Equip.
Pitchers	Food/Beverage—China
Plaster Repairs	POM—Building Supplies
Plates	Food/Beverage—China or Operating Supplies—Paper Supplies
Platters	Food/Beverage—China
Playing Cards	Rooms—Operating Supplies—Guest Supplies
Plumbing Repairs	POM—Elec. & Mech.
Polishes	F&B/Rooms—Operating Supplies—Cleaning Supplies
Pool—Accessories	POM—Swimming Pool
Pool—Chemicals	POM—Swimming Pool
Pool—Maintenance	POM—Swimming Pool
Pool—Repair	POM—Swimming Pool
Post Office Box Rental	A&G—Postage
Postage	A&G/Mktg.—Postage
Postage for Promotional Mailings	Mktg.—Adv.—Direct Mail
Postage Meter Rentals	A&G—Contract Services
Postcards (Guest)	Rooms—Operating Supplies—Guest Supplies
Posters—Safety	HR—Other (A&G—HR)
Presentation Binders	A&G—Operating Supplies & Equip.
Printed Forms	All Departments—Operating Supplies
Printer Supplies and Accessories	All Departments—Operating Supplies
Printing and Stationery	Rooms/Food/Beverage—Operating Supplies—Prtg. & Stat.; A&G/Telecommunications—Prtg. & Stat.
Printing Calculator	A&G—Operating Supplies & Equip.
Prizes—Employee	HR—Employee Relations (A&G—HR)
Professional Entertainers	Food/Beverage—Music & Entertainment
Programs	Food/Beverage—Music & Entertainment
Protective Service	Security—Contract Services (A&G—Security)
Protectors—Mattress	Rooms—Linen
Protest Fees	A&G—Professional Fees
Provision for Doubtful Accounts	A&G—Provision for Doubtful Accounts
Publications—House (for Employees)	HR—Employee Relations (A&G—Training)

Item	Classification
Public Liability Insurance	RPTI—Insurance—Liability
Public Rooms Cleaning (on Contract)— Banquet	Food/Beverage—Contract Services
Pump Repairs	POM—Elec. & Mech.

R

Item	Classification
Rack Cards	Rooms—Operating Supplies—Prtg.& Stat.
Ramekins	Food—China
Real Estate Rent (Land & Buildings)	RPTI—Rent—Land & Buildings
Real Estate Taxes	RPTI—Property Taxes—Real Estate Taxes
Record Books	Rooms/Food/Beverage—Operating Supplies—Prtg. & Stat.; A&G—Operating Supplies & Equip.
Recorders—Mini/Micro Cassette and Accessories	A&G—Operating Supplies & Equip.
Records	Food/Beverage—Music & Entertainment
Recycle Bins	A&G—Operating Supplies & Equip.
Refrigeration Supplies	POM—Other
Refuse Removal	POM—Removal of Waste Matter
Registered Cable/Telex Address	Mktg.—Selling—Other
Registration Cards	Rooms—Operating Supplies—Prtg. & Stat.
Removal of Ashes, Garbage, Rubbish, & Waste Matter	POM—Removal of Waste Matter
Rent—Building and Land	RPTI—Rent—Land & Buildings
Rent—Computer Equipment	RPTI—Rent—Information Systems Equip.
Rentals—Furniture for Public Rooms Banquet	Food/Beverage—Other
Rentals—Furniture for Public Rooms Non-Banquet	Rooms—Other
Rentals—Meters	POM—Other
Rentals—Tables	Rooms/Food/Beverage—Other
Replacement of Window Glass	POM—Building Supplies
Report Covers	A&G—Operating Supplies & Equip.
Reports	Rooms/Food/Beverage—Operating Supplies—Prtg. & Stat.; A&G—Operating Supplies & Equip.
Reservation Cards—Dining Room Tables .	Food—Operating Supplies
Reservation Expense	Rooms—Reservations
Reservation Forms	Rooms—Operating Supplies—Prtg. & Stat.
Restaurant Checks	Food/Beverage—Operating Supplies—Prtg. & Stat.
Restaurant Signs	Food—Other
Ribbons—Typewriter, Printing Calculator, Cash Register	A&G—Operating Supplies & Equip.
Ring Binders	A&G—Operating Supplies & Equip.
Royalties	Food/Beverage—Music & Entertainment

Item	Classification
Rubber Bands	Rooms/Food/Beverage—Operating Supplies—Prtg. & Stat.; A&G—Operating Supplies & Equip.
Rubber Stamps	Rooms/Food/Beverage—Operating Supplies—Prtg. & Stat.; A&G—Operating Supplies & Equip.

S

Item	Classification
Safe Deposit Box Keys	Rooms—Operating Supplies—Other
Safe Deposit Box Rentals (Off–site)	A&G—Other
Safety Matches (Guest)	Rooms/Food/Beverage—Operating Supplies—Guest Supplies
Sand—Fire Buckets	POM—Life/Safety
Saucers	Rooms/Food/Beverage—China
Scissors	Rooms/Food/Beverage—Operating Supplies—Prtg. & Stat.; A&G—Operating Supplies & Equip.
Scotch Tape	A&G—Operating Supplies & Equip.
Security—Contracted	Security—Contract Services (A&G—Security)
Server's Books	Food/Beverage—Operating Supplies—Prtg. & Stat.
Service Manuals (Employee)	All Departments—Training (HR—Training)
Serving Dishes	Rooms/Food/Beverage—China
Shampoo	Rooms—Operating Supplies—Guest Supplies; Health Center—Operating Supplies
Sheet Music	Food/Beverage—Music & Entertainment
Sheets—Linen	Rooms—Linen
Shoe Cloths	Rooms—Operating Supplies—Guest Supplies
Shortages and Overages—Cash	A&G—Cash Overages & Shortages
Signature Books	Food/Beverage—Operating Supplies—Prtg. & Stat.
Silver Cleaners	Food/Beverage—Operating Supplies—Cleaning Supplies
Soap Powders	Food/Beverage—Operating Supplies—Cleaning Supplies
Soaps	Rooms—Operating Supplies—Guest Supplies/Cleaning Supplies
Social & Sports Activities—Employees ...	HR—Employee Relations (A&G—HR)
Software—Application Upgrades	All Departments—Operating Supplies; Information Systems—Software—Commercial Applications (A&G—Information Systems)
Software Leases	Information Systems—Contract Services
Soufflé Cups	Food—Operating Supplies—Paper Supplies

Item	Classification
Souvenirs	Food/Beverage—Operating Supplies—Guest Supplies
Special Detective Service	Security—Contract Services (A&G—Security)
Spoons	Food/Beverage—China
Sports Activities & Equipment—Employees	HR—Employee Relations (A&G—HR)
Springs—Bed	POM—Furniture
Springs, Mattresses, and Pillow Repair	POM—Furniture
Stairway Repairs	POM—Building Supplies
Stamp Pads	Rooms/Food/Beverage—Operating Supplies—Prtg. & Stat.; A&G—Operating Supplies & Equip.
Stamps—General	A&G—Postage
Stamps—Selling	Mktg.—Selling—Postage
Staplers/Staples	Rooms/Food/Beverage—Operating Supplies—Prtg. & Stat.; A&G—Operating Supplies & Equip.
State Income Taxes	Federal & State Income Taxes
State Unemployment Taxes	PTEB—Payroll Taxes—State Unemployment
Stationery	Rooms/Food/Beverage—Operating Supplies—Prtg. & Stat.; A&G—Prtg. & Stat.
Stationery (Guest)	Rooms—Operating Supplies—Guest Supplies
Steel Wool	Rooms/Food/Beverage—Operating Supplies—Cleaning Supplies
Sticks—Swizzle	Food/Beverage—Operating Supplies—Paper Supplies
Stirrers for Glasses	Food/Beverage—Operating Supplies—Paper Supplies
Stock Pots—Repairs	POM—Elec. & Mech.
Stock Transfer Agents; Fees	A&G—Professional Fees
Stoppers	Food/Beverage—Operating Supplies
Stoppers—Tub	POM—Elec. & Mech.
Storage Files	A&G—Operating Supplies & Equip.
Storage of Equipment/Records (off-site)	A&G—Contract Services
Storeroom Issue Reports	Food/Beverage—Operating Supplies—Prtg. & Stat.
Storeroom Orders	Food/Beverage—Operating Supplies—Prtg. & Stat.
Strainers—Bars	Beverage—Operating Supplies—Other
Strainers—Beverages	Food—Operating Supplies—Utensils; Beverage—Operating Supplies—Other
Straws	Food/Beverage—Operating Supplies—Paper Supplies
Subscriptions—Mercantile Agencies	A&G—Dues & Subscriptions

Item	Classification
Subscriptions—Trade Publications	A&G/Mktg.—Dues & Subscriptions
Suggestion Awards—Employees	HR—Employee Relations (A&G—HR)
Surge Protectors	All Departments—Operating Supplies
Sweepers—Carpet	Rooms/Food/Beverage—Operating Supplies—Cleaning Supplies
Swim Suit Bags	Rooms—Operating Supplies—Guest Supplies
Swimming Pool Repairs	POM—Swimming Pool
Switchboard Repairs	POM—Elec. & Mech.

T

Item	Classification
Table Cloths/Protectors/Tops	Food/Beverage—China
Table Covers	POM—Furniture
Table Covers—Public Rooms Banquet	Food/Beverage—China
Table Pads	Food/Beverage—China
Table Protectors	Food/Beverage—China
Table Tent Cards	Food/Beverage—Operating Supplies—Prtg. & Stat.
Table Tops	Food/Beverage—China
Table Tops—Glass	POM—Furniture
Tags—Baggage	Rooms—Operating Supplies—Prtg. & Stat.
Tags—Laundry	House Laundry—Laundry Supplies
Tank—Toilet Floats	POM—Elec. & Mech.
Tape	POM—Other
Tape—Carpet	POM—Floor Covering
Tape—Masking	POM—Other
Tape Recorders	A&G—Operating Supplies & Equip.
Tape Transcribers	A&G—Operating Supplies & Equip.
Tapes (Cassette, etc.)	A&G—Operating Supplies & Equip.
Tax Stamp—Bond	Depr. & Amort.—Other
Taxes—Beverage—State (Not Included in Purchase Price)	Beverage—Cost of Beverage
Taxes—Franchise	Franchise Fees
Taxicab Fares	HR—Trans. (A&G—HR)
Teapots	Food/Beverage—China
Technical Books	All Departments—Training (A&G—Dues & Subscriptions)
Telephone Accessories—General	A&G—Communication Systems
Telephone Charges	All Departments—Telecommunications
Telephone Directories	Mktg.—Adv.—Media
Telephone Directory Advertising	Mktg.—Adv.—Media
Telephone Directory Covers and Holders .	A&G—Operating Supplies & Equip.
Telephone Equipment Charges	RPTI—Rent—Telecommunications Equip.
Telephone Lines—Computer Rentals	RPTI—Rent—Telecommunications Equip.
Telephone Rentals	RPTI—Rent—Telecommunications Equip.
Television Rentals	RPTI—Rent—Other

Item	Classification
Thread and Needles (Guest)	Rooms—Operating Supplies—Guest Supplies
Time Sharing Services	Information Systems—Other (A&G—Information Systems)
Timetables	Rooms—Operating Supplies
Toilet Items	Rooms—Operating Supplies—Guest Supplies
Toner (for copier)	A&G—Operating Supplies & Equip.
Total Quality Management	All Departments—Training
Tour Agency Commissions	Rooms—Commissions
Towels	Rooms—Linen; Food/Beverage—China
Trade Magazines & Publications Subscriptions	All Departments—Operating Supplies (A&G/Mktg./HR—Dues & Subscriptions)
Transfer Fees	A&G—Professional Fees
Transportation of Employees	HR—Trans. (A&G—Trans.)
Travel Agent Commissions	Rooms—Commissions
Traveling Expenses	A&G/Mktg.—Travel
Trays	Food/Beverage—China
Tumblers	Food/Beverage—China; Rooms—Operating Supplies

U

Item	Classification
Uncollectible Accounts	A&G—Provision for Doubtful Accounts (see also Balance Sheet—Allowance for Doubtful Accounts)
Uniforms	All Departments—Uniforms
Uniforms—Cleaning	Rooms/Food/Beverage/etc.—Uniforms or Other
Union (Trade) Insurance & Pension Fund (Employer's Contribution)	PTEB—Employee Benefits—Union Insurance; Union Pension
Utensils	Food—Operating Supplies—Utensils; Beverage—Operating Supplies—Other

V

Item	Classification
Vacuum Cleaner Accessories	Rooms/Food/Beverage—Operating Supplies—Cleaning Supplies
Visual Planners	A&G—Operating Supplies & Equip.
Vouchers	A&G—Operating Supplies & Equip.; Rooms/Food/Beverage—Operating Supplies—Prtg. & Stat.

W

Item	Classification
Want Ads (Help Wanted)	HR—Recruitment (A&G—HR)
Wastebaskets (Employee)	A&G—Operating Supplies & Equip.
Water	Utility Costs—Water

Item	Classification
Wax Paper	Food/Beverage—Operating Supplies—Paper Supplies
Window Shades—Contract Cleaning	Rooms—Contract Services
Window Shades, Screen, and Awning Repairs	POM—Curtains and Draperies
Wine Baskets	Beverage—Operating Supplies—Other
Wine Lists	Beverage—Operating Supplies—Prtg. & Stat.
Wired Music—Dining Rooms	Food/Beverage—Music & Entertainment
Wired Music—Lobby	Rooms—Other
Word Processor—Rental	RPTI—Rent—Information Systems Equip.
Workers' Compensation Insurance	PTEB—Employee Benefits—Workers' Compensation Insurance
Wrapping Paper (Laundry)	House Laundry—Laundry Supplies
Wrapping Paper and Twine	Rooms—Operating Supplies—Paper Supplies
Wringers and Mop Handles	Rooms/Food/Beverage—Operating Supplies—Cleaning Supplies
Writing Supplies	Rooms—Operating Supplies—Guest Supplies

Part V
Sample Set of Uniform
System Statements

SUMMARY STATEMENT OF INCOME

	NET REVENUES	COST OF SALES	PAYROLL AND RELATED EXPENSES	OTHER EXPENSES	INCOME (LOSS)
OPERATED DEPARTMENTS					
Rooms	$6,070,356		$1,068,383	$ 473,487	$4,528,486
Food	2,017,928	$ 733,057	617,705	168,794	498,372
Beverage	778,971	162,258	205,897	78,783	332,033
Telecommunications	213,744	167,298	31,421	17,309	-2,284
Rentals and Other Income	188,092				188,092
Total Operated Departments	9,269,091	1,062,613	1,923,406	738,373	5,544,699
UNDISTRIBUTED OPERATING EXPENSES					
Administrative and General			227,635	331,546	559,181
Marketing			116,001	422,295	538,296
Property Operation and Maintenance			204,569	163,880	368,449
Utility Costs				546,331	546,331
Total Undistributed Operating Expenses			548,205	1,464,052	2,012,257
TOTALS	$9,269,091	$1,062,613	$2,471,611	$2,202,425	3,532,442
INCOME AFTER UNDISTRIBUTED OPERATING EXPENSES					3,532,442
Rent, Property Taxes, and Insurance					641,029
INCOME BEFORE INTEREST, DEPRECIATION AND AMORTIZATION, AND INCOME TAXES					2,891,413
Interest Expense					461,347
INCOME BEFORE DEPRECIATION, AMORTIZATION AND INCOME TAXES					2,430,066
Depreciation and Amortization					552,401
GAIN ON SALE OF PROPERTY					1,574
INCOME BEFORE INCOME TAXES					1,879,239
Income Taxes					469,810
NET INCOME					$1,409,429

Rooms

	Current Period
REVENUE	$6,124,991
ALLOWANCES	54,635
NET REVENUE	6,070,356
EXPENSES	
Salaries and Wages	855,919
Employee Benefits	212,464
Total Payroll and Related Expenses	1,068,383
Other Expenses	
Cable/Satellite Television	20,100
Commissions	66,775
Complimentary Guest Services	2,420
Contract Services	30,874
Guest Relocation	1,241
Guest Transportation	48,565
Laundry and Dry Cleaning	42,495
Linen	12,140
Operating Supplies	122,600
Reservations	40,908
Telecommunications	12,442
Training	7,122
Uniforms	60,705
Other	5,100
Total Other Expenses	473,487
TOTAL EXPENSES	1,541,870
DEPARTMENTAL INCOME (LOSS)	$4,528,486

Food

	Current Period
TOTAL REVENUE	$2,017,928
REVENUE	$1,974,318
ALLOWANCES	7,864
NET REVENUE	1,966,454
COST OF SALES	
Cost of Food	743,260
Less Cost of Employee Meals	9,830
Less Food Transfers to Beverage	2,118
Plus Beverage Transfers to Food	1,035
Net Cost of Food	732,347
Other Cost of Sales	710
Total Cost of Sales	733,057
GROSS PROFIT (LOSS) ON FOOD SALES	1,233,397
OTHER INCOME	
Meeting Room Rentals	3,400
Miscellaneous Banquet Income	15,129
Service Charges	32,945
Total Other Income	51,474
GROSS PROFIT (LOSS) AND OTHER INCOME	1,284,871
EXPENSES	
Salaries and Wages	488,266
Employee Benefits	129,439
Total Payroll and Related Expenses	617,705
Other Expenses	
China, Glassware, Silver, and Linen	20,152
Contract Services	20,464
Laundry and Dry Cleaning	8,427
Licenses	1,300
Miscellaneous Banquet Expense	14,559
Music and Entertainment	4,618
Operating Supplies	57,512
Telecommunications	7,971
Training	8,400
Uniforms	15,200
Other	10,191
Total Other Expenses	168,794
TOTAL EXPENSES	786,499
DEPARTMENTAL INCOME (LOSS)	$ 498,372

Beverage

	Current Period
TOTAL REVENUE	$ 778,971
REVENUE	774,101
ALLOWANCES	4,618
NET REVENUE	769,483
COST OF SALES	
Cost of Beverage	160,905
Less Beverage Transfers to Food	1,035
Plus Food Transfers to Beverage	2,118
Net Cost of Beverage	161,988
Other Cost of Sales	270
Total Cost of Sales	162,258
GROSS PROFIT (LOSS) ON BEVERAGE SALES	607,225
OTHER INCOME	
Cover Charges	1,966
Service Charges	7,522
Total Other Income	9,488
GROSS PROFIT (LOSS) AND OTHER INCOME	616,713
EXPENSES	
Salaries and Wages	162,753
Employee Benefits	43,144
Total Payroll and Related Expenses	205,897
Other Expenses	
China, Glassware, Silver, and Linen	6,718
Contract Services	7,624
Gratis Food	1,914
Laundry and Dry Cleaning	3,088
Licenses	6,375
Music and Entertainment	18,975
Operating Supplies	14,200
Telecommunications	1,378
Training	3,600
Uniforms	7,830
Other	7,081
Total Other Expenses	78,783
TOTAL EXPENSES	284,680
DEPARTMENTAL INCOME (LOSS)	$ 332,033

Telecommunications

	Current Period
REVENUE	$214,810
ALLOWANCES	1,066
NET REVENUE	213,744
COST OF CALLS	
Long-Distance	124,966
Local	36,415
Utility Tax	4,602
Other	1,315
Total Cost of Calls	167,298
GROSS PROFIT (LOSS)	46,446
EXPENSES	
Salaries and Wages	25,566
Employee Benefits	5,855
Total Payroll and Related Expenses	31,421
Other Expenses	
Contract Services	6,250
Printing and Stationery	3,566
Telecommunications	1,714
Training	815
Other	4,964
Total Other Expenses	17,309
TOTAL EXPENSES	48,730
DEPARTMENTAL INCOME (LOSS)	$ (2,284)

Administrative and General

	Current Period
PAYROLL AND RELATED EXPENSES	
Salaries and Wages	$ 182,108
Employee Benefits	45,507
Total Payroll and Related Expenses	227,635
OTHER EXPENSES	
Bank Charges	2,115
Cash Overages and Shortages	816
Communication Systems	8,454
Contract Services	1,609
Credit and Collection	15,746
Credit Card Commissions	62,906
Donations	10,000
Dues and Subscriptions	7,283
Head Office	8,919
Human Resources	30,349
Information Systems	12,140
Internal Audit	3,600
Internal Communications	7,400
Loss and Damage	1,615
Meals and Entertainment	3,200
Operating Supplies and Equipment	15,914
Postage	7,421
Printing and Stationery	8,972
Professional Fees	4,619
Provision for Doubtful Accounts	22,406
Security	42,911
Telecommunications	15,841
Training	7,500
Transportation	3,918
Travel	14,200
Other	11,692
Total Other Expenses	331,546
TOTAL ADMINISTRATIVE AND GENERAL EXPENSES	$ 559,181

Marketing

	Current Period
SELLING	
PAYROLL AND RELATED EXPENSES	
Salaries and Wages	$ 57,658
Employee Benefits	14,415
Total Payroll and Related Expenses	72,073
OTHER EXPENSES	
Complimentary Guests	1,562
Contract Services	1,815
Dues and Subscriptions	6,679
Meals and Entertainment	7,482
Printing and Stationery	8,419
Postage	5,900
Trade Shows	12,500
Telecommunications	12,213
Training	3,347
Travel	16,424
Other	7,172
Total Other Expenses	84,513
TOTAL SELLING EXPENSES	156,586
ADVERTISING AND MERCHANDISING	
PAYROLL AND RELATED EXPENSES	
Salaries and Wages	35,128
Employee Benefits	8,800
Total Payroll and Related Expenses	43,928
OTHER EXPENSES	
Collateral Material	28,793
Contract Services	4,916
Direct Mail	77,398
Frequent Stay Programs	25,941
In-House Graphics	36,223
Media	102,059
Outdoor	15,914
Point-of-Sale Material	9,286
Telecommunications	6,014
Other	4,615
Total Other Expenses	311,159
TOTAL ADVERTISING AND MERCHANDISING EXPENSES	355,087
FEES AND COMMISSIONS	
Agency Fees	5,574
Other	649
Total Fees and Commissions	6,223
OTHER MARKETING EXPENSES	20,400
TOTAL MARKETING EXPENSES	$ 538,296

Property Operation and Maintenance

	Current Period
PAYROLL AND RELATED EXPENSES	
Salaries and Wages	$ 163,899
Employee Benefits	40,670
Total Payroll and Related Expenses	204,569
OTHER EXPENSES	
Building Supplies	12,460
Contract Services	10,100
Curtains and Draperies	3,415
Electrical and Mechanical Equipment	4,892
Elevators	10,619
Engineering Supplies	10,117
Floor Covering	12,924
Furniture	15,141
Grounds and Landscaping	6,152
Heating, Ventilating, and Air Conditioning Equipment	6,967
Kitchen Equipment	2,015
Laundry Equipment	1,914
Life/Safety	4,570
Light Bulbs	3,418
Locks and Keys	2,618
Operating Supplies	6,529
Painting and Decorating	8,915
Removal of Waste Matter	10,996
Swimming Pool	5,602
Telecommunications	6,118
Training	3,441
Uniforms	2,615
Vehicle Maintenance	8,911
Other	3,431
Total Other Expenses	163,880
TOTAL PROPERTY OPERATION AND MAINTENANCE EXPENSES	$ 368,449

Utility Costs

	Current Period
UTILITY COSTS	
Electricity	$ 226,514
Gas	236,100
Oil	8,500
Water	62,524
Other Fuels	13,053
Total Utility Costs	$ 546,331